Zensho W. Kopp
The Direct Zen Way to Liberation

AF284068

Zensho W. Kopp

The Direct Zen Way
to Liberation

With 50 abstract drawings by the author

This book is the extended version of the audio book that was published by Amazon Publishing under the same name.
In their letters to the author, many listeners expressed the wish to have the audio recording in book form so that they may delve more deeply into its profound wisdom.
This wish has now led to the text at hand, together with Zen Master Zensho's detailed "Introduction to the essence and practice of Zen."

Visit our website at
http://www.tao-chan.org/

Bibliographic information from the German National Library:
The German National Library lists this publication in the German National Bibliography; detailed bibliographic data is available online at dnb.dnb.de.

© 2015 Zenso W. Kopp

Publisher: BoD · Books on Demand GmbH, Überseering 33, 22297 Hamburg, bod@bod.de
Printed by: Libri Plureos GmbH, Friedensallee 273, 22763 Hamburg

Original title "Der direkte Zen Weg zur Befreiung"
Translation: John Kitching
Cover design / Print optimisation: Jörg Zimmermann
Photo back cover: Verena Kopp
Drawings: Zensho W. Kopp
Typesetting: Torsten Zander
ISBN 978-3-7526-4115-8

When you let your mind drop headlong into the fathomless depths where intellect and thinking can never reach, you will behold the absolute, radiating One Mind. This is how you achieve liberation from the cycle of birth and death.

Zen Master Ta-hui (12th century)

Inhalt

Preface

Exceptionally clear in their directness, the statements in this book are filled with the profound wisdom of Zen. They hold within them such spiritual brilliance that they can touch us at our very core.

Here, the logic of our deep-rooted intellectual thinking is often shattered and an opportunity arises for us to intuitively grasp the truth, which is incomprehensible to the intellect.

In a modern and refreshingly unconventional way, Zen Master Zensho teaches a Zen way that is completely free and not bound to any special form. Thus in this book we find alongside the many Zen-quotes, numerous quotes from Indian Vedanta and Christian mysticism too.

What is special about Zensho's teaching methods is that he comes directly to the point, without any sonorous digressions, and that he points to the essence. Thus, his arousing words in this book are also a complete rebellion against our conditioned intellect, for they smash all our fixed concepts and tender illusions. With Zenistic consistency, everything is swept away so that we become able to reach liberation of the mind beyond our limited intellectual logic and can experience a state of pure awareness.

For Zensho, from the first page to the last, it is a question of our awakening from the everyday slumber of our habits, which prevent us from directly experiencing reality. Zensho says:

Therefore, it is essential in Zen to realise absolute awareness Now-Here, from moment to moment, wherever we are and in everything we do. The truth of Zen is simple and direct. Indeed it can be seen in the most commonplace things of everything life.

The reality we are seeking is constantly present – right now in this instant! In drinking a glass of water or tying shoelaces the mystery and marvel of Zen reveals itself. Yet this can only be understood and experienced by those people who live life in the complete presence of the immediate moment.

A wonderful example of this can be found in Zensho's drawings in this book, drawn with great spontaneity and absolute awareness, which directly express the Zen mind. Zen is solely based on experiencing. Thus, all the great masters of Zen warn us over and over again of making Zen the object of logical, rational speculation, since we cannot master the truth of Zen through concepts, teachings or philosophies.

For this reason, theoretical interpretations of Buddhist teachings in Zen are compared to a finger that points to the moon. However, if we wish to see the moon, we must not remain caught up in viewing the finger pointing to the moon in the mistaken assumption that the finger itself is the moon. Instead we must detach ourselves from the finger and view the moon itself.

With brilliant clarity, Zensho shows us the way to liberation from our self-impeding thought-compulsion and our conditioned patterns of feelings and behaviour that darken our true perspective and make our lives sorrowful and unfree. And so with the aid of many citations, he lets the old Chinese Zen masters have their say, who, with their paradox words and actions, unhinge our intellect.

For example, a quote from classic Zen literature of one of the old masters or one of their Mondos – a dialogue between master and student – is examined and illuminated.

These elucidating explanations provide the essential key to understanding the sayings. Without these explanations by a master who abides in the same enlightened consciousness dimension as these old Chinese masters, the profound content of these sayings would remain concealed – especially those "nimble-witted" dialogues between master and student in which in an often rough and ready way the deadlocked thinking of the Zen student is shattered.

Of high value for this book is Zensho's extensive introduction in "The essence and practice of Zen," which provides the reader with a compact summary of Zen practice. In this very lively Zen book with Zensho's expressive drawings, which breathe the spirit of Zen, we feel the realisation and freedom of one of the most important wisdom teachers of our times. He possesses the special gift of imparting the profound truth of Zen in a contemporary way. Zensho language is refreshingly true-to-life and of a striking clarity that transforms and liberates us.

In a simple way, he shows us the path to fulfilling our true being that can be practised in the midst of daily life in our modern world. All those who believe they must distance themselves from everyday life on the spiritual path will be quickly set right of their mistaken notions in this book. Zensho's direct Zen way to liberation is "radically empirical". It is not a way of world-fleeing elitist seclusion but rather; it leads us through the midst of the world.

May 2015   Zen Center Tao Chan, Wiesbaden

Some remarks on the drawings

The special value and uniqueness of the collection of drawings in Zensho's book is that they are revelations in pictorial form of an enlightened consciousness. Far from all traditional confinement, the Zen Master and artist Zensho W. Kopp goes his own individual way by not painting with black tusche as is common in Zen art but by creating pencil drawings.

Zensho's drawings, which breathe the true Zen mind, are reflections of his innermost being that have become visible. His artistic way of expression corresponds to that of the old Chinese and Japanese Zen painters, who, with few strokes and often downright tumultuous brush use, knew how to express the bare essentials. Zensho's spontaneous art of painting, along with the abstract forms of his drawings, express the spirit of Zen in a way that is not possible through words.

Thus we feel that something intangible moves us from within the subtle tension affinities of his drawings – between line and white background, between form and formlessness. The forms appear to float away dematerialised, to be preserved in the empty depths of transcendent, otherworldly spheres.

Thus, the empty background in Zensho's paintings is much more than just an unpainted part of the picture.

In Zen painting, the empty background relates to the empty base of being, and represents the form- and featureless void, Sunyata. This empty base is that absolute reality that shines through the transparency of all forms and colours, and thus all phenomena.

Here too, the profound meaning of the omissions and areas left empty can be seen in the master's paintings. The reduction of the appearances to their essence is the core of Zensho's artwork. It does not deal with phenomena perceived by the senses, but rather with that absolute reality that lies behind everything. In Zen painting, this highest reality of all is expressed by the circular symbol "Enso". It is the best known symbol of Zen, which we find again and again in Zensho's drawings. In these drawings, characterised by atmospheric clarity, the essence of a spiritual master is expressed, who, having awoken to the reality of Being, has experienced the harmony and totality of the universe, which underlies everything. Immersed in silent contemplation of these images, a new, unimagined insight opens to us into the reality of our true being. For that which the artist and mystic has imbued into his images, gushes forth from them and flows with irresistible force into our mind.

Zen Master Zensho's drawings in this book are true masterpieces of artistic creativity. Whoever immerses themselves in these revelations of the invisible which have entered into the realm of the visible, likewise immerses themselves in that reality from which they have emerged.

May 2015   Edward Duvernoy

Introduction
to the essence and practice of Zen

Instantly grasping reality

The main objective of Zen is the awakening to the reality of our true being. Zen points constantly and with great emphasis to the One Mind as our original, true essence, and at the same time is an entirely practical teaching, completely oriented to the reality of here and now. The method of its spiritual conveyance is strikingly simple and instantly direct. For this reason, Zen puts all frills aside and points solely to absolute reality, which reveals itself Now-Here.

Zen is the height and the quintessence of the whole of Buddhism. Although it originated from Buddhism, it quickly turned away from traditional Buddhism, for Zen is not at all interested in the high philoso-phical speculations of Buddhist erudition. Quite the con-trary – it much rather endeavours to consistently break with discursive rational thinking, which is constantly trying to define and thus limit everything that belongs to the realm of the unfathomable. The Chinese Zen Master Ying-an (twelfth century) says of this:

> The truth of Zen cannot be gained through lectures, debates and explanations. If at some point you suddenly turn the light of your mind around and see through all deceptions, you will perceive the true Self.

This is the original, vivacious Zen of instantly grasping reality, just as it was practised by the great Chinese masters during the Golden Age of Zen. It sets itself apart through its radical independence and teaches a direct path to liberation in a refreshingly lively way that is not attached to any form. One of the principle characteristics of Zen is its special way of conveyance beyond all holy Buddhist scriptures and words.

All discriminating, intellectual thinking is a fundamental barrier on the path to enlightenment for the Zen-Buddhist devotee. This is why Zen offers no particular teaching and no ready-made answers. It eludes our reasoning and defies all conceptual denomination. Thus Bodhidharma, the legendary first patriarch of Zen from the sixth century declares:

My teaching penetrates directly into a person's heart. Therefore it is unique and not entangled in words and canonical regulations; it is the direct transfer of the true seal.

Zen cannot be learnt nor studied, for it does not allow itself to be understood by the limited one-sidedness of the ego-centred intellect. Those who wish to learn Zen are on the wrong path right from the beginning. You can have studied Zen Buddhism exhaustively and know everything about it yet what use are all these empty words if you do not recognise your own, true being?

Zen leads us past the world of the intellect to a reality that has always been there: vivacious, omnipresent and free from abstraction. Using the logic of discriminating, conceptual thinking to fathom the ultimate truth is in the eyes of Zen ignorance, for relying on our intellectual understanding means preventing the inner light of our true Self from unfolding.

The true Self-Mind, beside which nothing else exists, is the empty, radiating nature of being. This mind is by its very nature without substance and omnipresent. It is our absolute reality, which reveals itself "Now-Here". Everything that appears before our eyes as the myriad forms is the reflection of this One Mind.

There is no existence and no non-existence of the phenomena. Appearance and reality pervade each other completely. This is the central message of Zen.

For this reason it is also written in the Mahaprajnapa-ramita Hridaya Sutra, also known as the "Heart-Sutra" for short, which is recited daily in Zen monasteries, "Form is emptiness and emptiness is form." An intuitive understanding of this "Mind-only-teaching," with an unshakeable belief in the original purity of the mind is seen in Zen as the essential prerequirement for reaching enlightenment.

There is nothing which could not be holy. Ultimately, this means, "nothing is holy". In the words of Bodhidharma in his answer to the question: what is the holiest in the world, he replied, "Boundless openness – nothing holy!"

Zen is a pure matter of personal experience. Therefore it wants to and must be lived, everywhere and at all times, in each instant of the day, for the present moment encompasses everything, the entire fullness of being. If we miss the present moment, we miss out on true life since we miss omnipresent divine reality.

The sword of wisdom

In the direct presence of Now we abide in the timeless eternity of being. Therefore, we must experience the present moment in crystal-clear consciousness and as constantly new by completely immersing ourselves in it – free from all notions and concepts.

We must truly experience the truth of Zen in its entirety and inwardly absorb and live it with our whole being. Yet, since we are unable to grasp the unspeakable, profound mystery of Zen with our thinking, we require the wordless initiation of an enlightened master so that our inner eye of perception opens. This takes place in the tradition of Zen in a direct, secret transfer from Heart-Mind to Heart-Mind. For this reason, the Chinese Zen Master Huang-po (ninth century) says:

> There is no understanding through words, just a transfer from mind to mind.

In their powerful, direct way of conveyance, the masters warn their students over and over again not to cling to words, since the highest truth cannot be spoken, has never been spoken, and will never be spoken. The highest truth is dynamic and vivacious, whereas our concepts are static and dead. Therefore, Zen calls on us to liberate our mind from everything – whatever it may be, and not to rely on any artificial methods of reaching the truth. So follow this viewpoint and grasp the sword of non-discriminating wisdom and shatter right now, in this instant, the chains of your intellectual interpretations. In the powerful words of Zen Master Hsueh-tou:

> Where the sword of wisdom flies, sun and moon lose their shine and heaven and earth lose their colour. Through this experience the devils' bellies burst and the eye of transcendental wisdom opens to you.

Zen is not a matter of learning but rather of un-learning. It is a returning to the origin of our true being. This means we must completely leave behind us all our illusory knowledge and the knowledge of Zen and Buddhism we have accumulated up to now if we wish to achieve sublime enlightenment. At the most, one could concede that these teachings have a guiding, preparatory value. Yet in the eyes of the great old Chinese Zen Masters like Lin-chi, Ma-tsu, Hui-neng and Huang-po, all the scriptures of traditional Buddhism were just worthless paper. The Chinese

Zen Master Yung-chia (eighth century) is of the same opinion:

Directly cutting off the roots, that is the Buddha's seal. I do not care about collecting leaves and seeking twigs.

If we truly wish to experience the profound truth of Zen, we must immerse ourselves in it directly and avoid becoming separated from reality through concepts and ideas. In the language of Zen: "Where nothing is sought, the unborn Self-Mind is present." For this reason, Zen masters do not give explanations and define nothing, for defining means setting limits.

The Self-Mind is Buddha

With the greatest emphasis, Zen constantly points to the "Heart-Mind" as our true essential nature, so that we become able to discover the truth within ourselves and awaken to our original buddha-nature. Indeed, it is completely impossible to find the Self-Mind, that is, our true Self, anywhere else than in our own mind. We can search externally as much as we like yet how could we possibly find ourselves when we look anywhere other than in ourselves? The Chinese Zen Master Yuan-wu (twelfth century) says of this:

The great truth of Zen is in everyone's possession. Just look into your own, true essence and do not seek it through others. Your own mind is beyond all forms, it is free and silent and self-sufficient. Perpetually it reveals itself. In its light everything dissolves.

Zen Master Yuan-wu gives us this good piece of advice: "Just look into your own, true essence." This well-intentioned advice points to Zen meditation practice as an essential element of Zen. Even though this is so, nowadays most adherents of Zen Buddhism occupy themselves only theoretically with the teachings of Zen. That is a very sad state. Without the clarity of mind accomplished in Zen meditation, it is not possible to liberate oneself from the dualism of discriminating, conceptual thinking, which, like dark clouds, covers the light of our true Self. This is why the Chinese Zen Master Hung-chi (twelfth century) says:

To experience Zen in its complete profound-ness, you must clear the mind and immerse yourself in the silent practice of inward percep-tion. If you gain fully unlimited insight into the origin of reality, the mind is open, clear and bright like the moon, which takes away the darkness of night. Completely whole, radiating in light, it lights up the entire universe and cuts through past, present and future.

Zen meditation is the absolute prerequisite for enlightenment. Therefore it is viewed in Zen Buddhism as an essential practice on our path to realisation. Yet once our inner eye of enlightenment has opened, meditation will no longer be any special practice, for it will now become a totally natural and spontaneous expression of our daily life. Whether we are sitting or standing, wherever we are and whatever we do, everything becomes wonderful meditation.

In this consciousness state of effortless, easeful awareness of mind we are in the all-embracing wholeness of being and experience ourselves as One with all beings. Zen Master Fen-yan (eleventh century) provides us with an excellent description of this high Zen-realisation that follows enlightenment:

When Zen becomes your natural life, your mind remains composed and is not roused by worldly matters. You are in the realm of enlightenment, you transcend the ordinary world and are completely free in the midst of the masses. Thus you are in complete unity with that which is beyond the world, and at the same time you embrace that which is in the realm of the existent. The words spoken here refer to that absolute realisation in which the Mumonkan, "The Gateless Gate" to boundless liberation has truly been surpassed. We only have great liberation when we have truly experienced profound Satori – great enlightenment, and not just a fleeting glimpse of our essential nature. Yet although Satori is experienced in an instant, this enlightened consciousness of radiating clarity must be stabilised over a long period of time in everyday life. Only then do we achieve Hum-realisation in the midst of the world.

This realised, crystal-clear consciousness can no longer be lost. Our whole essence has been transformed so that our entire life has become an experience of the all-embracing wholeness of being. Here, we experience Samsara and Nirvana as an inseparable entity.

Koan practice

A further essential element in Zen besides meditation is "koan" study. A koan is a paradox, a spiritual problem that the student receives from his master and whose solution is not possible by means of discriminating thought. It is a practical and very elaborate means that the old Chinese masters created to help us in our efforts towards enlightenment.

The great Chinese masters of the Golden Age of Zen were very creative minds who had the ability to spontaneously bring forth koans, which were adapted to the individual consciousness-state of their students. One of the best known koans is the following one from the Mumonkan, the "Gateless gate," a koan collection from the thirteenth century by the Chinese Zen Master Mumon:

> It is just like the Zen monk, hanging by his teeth from the branch of a tall tree with nothing else to support him. His hands cannot grasp the branch; his feet cannot touch the tree. A passing traveller comes to a halt beneath the tree and asks him, "Why did Bodhidharma come from the West?" (This question, often asked in Zen in fact means: "What is the profound meaning of the truth of Zen?")
> If he does not answer, he will not fulfil the Buddhist vow of helping all beings reach liberation. Yet if he answers, he will lose his life. What should he do?

To this end, the Chinese Zen Master Mumon provides the following commentary:

Although your eloquence flows like a river, it does not help you at all here. Even if you can recite the entire collection of Buddhist sutras it is of no value either. Yet if you can truly answer, you will kill the living and bring the dead to life.

The following koan is found in the Mumonkan too and is considered in Zen as one of the eight most difficult ones:

A cow goes through a window. Its head, its horns, its belly and its four legs are already through. How can it then be that the tail does not go through?

At the abyss of the void

A koan is no puzzle, we cannot solve it since it has no possibility of a solution as does a puzzle, by which we just have to find the correct answer. A true Zen koan is insoluble, we cannot solve it; we can only "dissolve" it. And since we cannot solve a koan there is only one way out:

We must awaken from our dream of body, mind and

world and thus "dissolve" the illusion of our attachment to the cycle of birth and death. This means: the answer to the koan lies within us, for the koan solely involves us and no one else.

The striking feature of all koans is their alogical nature – the absurdity of the words and actions. The answers of the Zen masters to their students' questions emanate from the Zen mind. On reading these answers, confusion arises and one asks oneself what the answer has actually to do with the question.

However, we should make it clear to ourselves that these statements of the great Zen masters have nothing to do with any conceptual or intellectual assertation within the usual bounds of our logical thinking. Instead we are dealing with the manifestation of a tremendous experience of such all-encompassing universality that within it, all barriers of space and time and all limitations of verbal communication are transcended.

The koan overwhelms our intellect. It causes a short circuit in our thinking and paralyses our capacity for critical discernment. For the intent and purpose of a koan is that it brings us into a spiritual borderline situation in which our intellect is trapped and we can neither move forwards nor backwards. We find ourselves faced with the abyss of the void and our only salvation is to let go of ourselves and everything, whatever it may be. In the words of the Chinese Zen Master Ta-hui from the twelfth century:

> If you allow your mind to abruptly sink into the unfathomable depths that intellect and thought can never penetrate, you will behold the absolute, radiating One Mind. This is how you achieve liberation from the cycle of birth and death.

Essential when dealing with a koan is that we achieve that crystal-clear consciousness state from out of which the words were spoken, and which logical analysis can never reach. Only when the mind is mature enough that it is completely akin to the mind of the master who gave us the koan will the profound truth disclose itself to us that was concealed in the koan.

The master

A true master will never offer his student an answer to a koan. In doing so he would deprive him of the opportunity of experiencing the manifestation of the hidden truth within the koan that reveals itself to him in a sudden inner explosion of recognition.

The principle function of a Zen master is much rather in removing all obstacles that separate us from directly experiencing the truth. With tender harshness he shatters with the sword of non-discriminating wisdom the whole forest of concepts that darken our mind like a dense, creeping tangle.

His efforts, which are often of a physical nature, have the sole purpose of revealing what from the beginning onwards has been present in our innermost self as our true essence. The following example elucidates this:

> The Chinese Zen Master Yun-men (tenth century) entered the Dharma hall and said: "Buddha achieved enlightenment when the morning star appeared."
>
> To this a monk asked, "What is it like to achieve enlightenment when the morning star appears?"
>
> Yun-men replied, "Come here and I'll show you!"
>
> The monk went up to him. The master hit him with his staff and chased him out of the Dharma hall.

A master will make use of all available means, be it loud cries or blows with a stick, to burst open the deluded mind and to awaken us from the slumber of our habitual views and perspectives. For Each habitual, conditioned viewpoint, in whichever form it may be, prevents us from directly experiencing reality.

Satori – great enlightenment

There is no gradual enlightenment, instead just a sudden awakening to the reality of our true being. This is the essential, core concept of Zen. Enlightenment does not have different steps and it happens very suddenly, but in general only at the end of a long process of spiritual maturation.

Satori, the great enlightenment experience, is like the blossoming of a lotus flower. It is akin to the sudden awakening of a dreamer. It always comes over us in a flash and completely unexpectedly, for it is an absolute moment-experience.

However, in order to reach this experience we must firstly achieve a state of total relinquishment. We are only mature enough for liberation from our bound state in the cycle of birth and death when we have given up our habitual attachments to our concepts.

In this spiritual state of disengagement from body, mind and world, we reach the threshold of mystical death. The ego dies the "great death," and what follows is the "great life". We experience our resurrection above the dark mists of phenomena into the clear light of reality. Our true eye of enlightenment is suddenly opened and just like one who has risen from the dead, we will break out in laughter and clap our hands for joy.

We will immediately recognise that our own mind and the boundless expanse of the One Mind are a single being, beside which nothing else exists. In this great liberation, the ups and downs of everyday life no longer have any power over our consciousness. The chains of illusion are broken and we have entered into a higher world of reality. In its manner of absolute directness, Zen always points to the fact that enlightenment is possible for anyone at any time who is absolutely prepared to completely give up himself and all his fixed concepts. Zen Master Shen-tsang (eighth century) describes this as follows:

Unparalleled the wonderful light shines, inexpressible in words and letters. As soon as you just let your delusions fall, Buddhahood becomes reality.

At this moment of great liberation our original true being, the One Mind reveals itself, which was concealed behind the dark clouds of discriminating, conceptual thinking. Zen Master Huang-po (ninth century) describes this wonderful experience in the following words:

> This pure Mind, the source of everything, shines forever and on all with the brilliance of its own perfection. But the people of the world do not awake to it, regarding only that which sees, hears, feels and knows as mind. Blinded by their own sight, hearing, feeling and knowing, they do not perceive the spiritual brilliance of the source-substance.
>
> If they would finally throw off all conceptual thought in a flash this source-substance would manifest itself like the sun ascending through the void and illuminating the whole universe without hindrance or bounds.

In the powerful words of the Chinese Zen Master Fa-yong from the twelfth century:

> The power of non-thinking is like the embers of the flame or the lightening-fast blow of a sharp sword. The moment the mind is free of thoughts, the lion's roar is reached. All further

description would only place lesser minds in fear and confusion.

The dark clouds of our spiritual ignorance disappear in this liberation from the chains of our self-caused limitations. The mind radiates like the clear sky in boundless openness and emptiness, and nothing can darken it any longer. The reality of our original, true being lies within ourselves. There is nothing to achieve and nothing to change. Our true Self is already absolutely consummate right now and has always been so.

By recognising that the own mind as our true being is buddha, and neither begins with birth nor perishes with death, the mystery of Zen reveals itself. That is why Zen places the highest importance on the insight that enlightenment is indwelling in the mind and so there is nothing to achieve. The direct experience of the truth of Zen is by reaching the original state of the mind and is thus freedom from all limitations and illusions.

It is completely clear to me that some of what is written in this book will be challenging and startling for the reader. Much of what they are convinced of and believe in will be laid bare and swept away. However, this is intended to be so.

Not for nothing is it said in Zen: "The Zen path to liberation is no path for small minds." For only he who is truly prepared to leave behind his accustomed perspectives and liberate himself from all concepts will be mature enough for the transformation into the highest consciousness level of the boundless liberation of the mind.

Wiesbaden, Germany, Spring 2015
Zensho W. Kopp

Chapter 1

The Search for Truth

The inner calling

Everything that has a beginning is subject to the law of impermanence simply "because" it has a beginning. Thus, human life too undergoes the process of birth and death. It is subject to the continual process of transformation: arising – subsiding, arising – subsiding.

And so we ask ourselves: "Is that really all there is? Surely somewhere there must be something lasting." And just this alone; our desire for stability, security and bliss is a constant inner calling and indication of the presence of a higher reality.

Thus we start to seek, without knowing "what" we are actually seeking. Yet what we seek is in truth nothing other than our true divine Self. It is our own reality. We have never lost it, it is there and it has always been there. It is just that we have covered it with the projections of our discriminating, conceptual thinking so that we have forgotten who and what we really are.

Yet now, right here, in this instant, the reality of our true being reveals itself – nothing could be closer. If we do not find it here we will find it nowhere. In the words of Zen Master Lin-chi from the ninth century:

> You wear down your feet rushing in all directions. What are you actually seeking? There is no buddha to seek externally.

It is paradoxical that the truth has always been present and attainable, yet it withdraws itself as soon as we deliberately try to grasp it. The truth of Zen is directly before us but as soon as we start reflecting on it we fall into disarray.

When we interpret things with our intellect we

become more and more distant from the reality we are seeking for we remain solely within our self-made limitations of dualistic discrimination. In this way we embroil ourselves ever deeper in the creeping tangle of our discriminating, conceptual thinking. But Zen rises above all this and calls to us:

> If you could only free yourself from conceptual thinking you would recognise that there is no other buddha than the one in your own mind.

These words by Zen Master Huang-po from the ninth century form the core of the true, original Zen of the ancient Chinese masters. We are only truly on the path to liberation when we can prevent our thoughts from roaming and seeking. When we try to grasp Zen with concepts, we create our own restrictions and fall short of reality.

"All conceptual thinking is a mistaken opinion," says Zen. So why stuff your brain with all sorts of intellectual rubbish? What is the point of rooting around in every corner like a dog scraping up all kinds of old rubbish in its muzzle? Instead, let us dig into our own treasure, for the truth we are seeking is closer to us than we are to ourselves.

There is nothing to seek, there is nothing to gain!

There is no space in which things could be separate from one another, and there is no time in which anything is yet to appear or is no longer there. For everything takes place simultaneously, by which all things mutually permeate one another.

Everything is an all-encompassing whole that contains everything within it Now-Here. And since everything is Now-Here, where will we seek and what will we seek? When we wish to experience our true, original being, there is no other way than to immerse ourselves in it Now-Here. How can we experience what is here right now when we are caught in tomorrow or the day after or when we are anywhere else than here?

Silent perception

If we wish to perceive our true being, it is absolutely necessary that we penetrate through and cast off the subjective projections of our own mind. It is equally necessary for us to give up our exclusive trust in our acquired knowledge and understanding.

This means we must completely rid ourselves of our trust in our perception of the world through conceptual definition. Thus, transform your desire for rational understanding into silent inner perception, free of intellectual speculation. Cast doubt on all religious and philosophical beliefs! They are nothing more than interpretations of the neurotic intellect. Therefore, we do not need to believe in any religious dogmas. The old Chinese Zen masters constantly pointed with great emphasis to the fact that on the Zen path there is nothing to achieve and nothing to learn. There is nothing to reach and there is no holy truth to realise.

Rid yourself of all concepts! Completely break free

from all forms of limitation and everything that can be explained! The truth of our true being can never be made the object of logical, rational explanations. The ancient Chinese Zen masters had their own special way of making this clear to their students:

45

On one occasion, news spread throughout the land that Zen Master Huang-po planned to deliver a great public dharma sermon on the truth of Zen and that all monks from neighbouring monasteries were invited to attend. The monks came from everywhere, from near and far. The great dharma hall was hardly big enough to accommodate the many eagerly waiting listeners.

Then the big moment came. The bell was sounded and Zen Master Huang-po entered the dharma hall and sat down on his high seat. After a moment's silence he began:

"Having many sorts of knowledge cannot be compared with giving up seeking for anything. This is the best of all things! Mind is not of several kinds and there is no doctrine that can be put into words. And as there is no more to be said, the assembly is dismissed!"

Having spoken these impressive words, Zen Master Huang-po stepped down from his high seat and left the dharma hall.

Chapter 2

The Great Trust-Awakening

Inner transformation

The truth we seek is within us. At the same time it is also directly before us and reveals itself in all phenomena. Everything – sun, moon, stars and sky, the earth and all beings – is the One Mind, beside which nothing else exists. Everything is the One Mind and the external world is its revelation. This can be seen in the following story:

One day, a monk came to the Chinese Zen Master Tsao-shan, who lived in the ninth century, and asked him:

> "What of the appearances is true?"
> Tsao-shan said, "Appearance is truth and truth is appearance."
> The monk did not understand and continued, "And where is this revealed?"
> "Here!" said the master, raising the tea tray into the air.

Everything is the reality of the One Mind. There is nothing that exists which is not a phenomenon of reality. Yet we superimpose these phenomena with the notion of multiplicity and separateness.

However, we will not find any inner peace until Ultimate Reality reveals itself within us as the origin and aim of all life. This will only take place when we awaken from the dream of an apparent, multitudinous world.

This experience of our true, divine being will only be bestowed on us when we are prepared to free ourselves of our false notions. This means letting go of all our habitual behaviour patterns and ways of thinking and thus letting go of ourselves. We can only achieve liberation when we have let go of our "self," that is, what we believe we are. Then peace and the fullness of Divine Being will be accorded to us in the mind-state of "inner detachment". Only then will we achieve that solitude that represents far more than just "externally" letting go since it effectuates an "inner" transformation. The Christian Mystic Meister Eckhart from the fourteenth century gives us the following advice:

> Firstly you should forsake "yourself," then you
> have forsaken everything. Indeed, were a man

to forsake a kingdom or the whole world, but would retain himself, so would he have forsaken nothing. Yet were he to leave off from himself, then whatever he may keep, be it riches or otherwise, he will indeed have forsaken everything.

Without our trust in the reality of Divine Being we will never achieve such inner disengagement. However, we are not talking here about pseudo-trust in the sense of taking something to be true on a superficial, intellectual level. Instead, we are talking about that particular trust which is an irrefutable inner certitude of the soul. It is the inner certitude that remains, even when no enduring belief is present in your thoughts, and even then when the intellect rebels, refuses and doubts everything.

Trusting of the heart

All those who make serious efforts on the spiritual path also know the varying periods of disappointment, darkness, and wavering belief. Yet at the same time there is something there that abides with us and remains, despite all doubt. It is that something that tells us in our innermost self that what we have turned to is nonetheless true. However, this trust is not the wavering trust of the beginner on the spiritual path but rather that "great trust," which has first to develop.

When you have seriously followed the spiritual path for a long time, this unswerving trust within your heart will remain despite all internal and external challenges. Even when such trust may appear to the mistrusting intellect as blind trust, it is nevertheless endlessly wiser that any human intelligence, caught in logical thinking.

Through this great trust we reach that inner detachment which leads us from the limiting, grasping ego-awareness to our original identity within our true

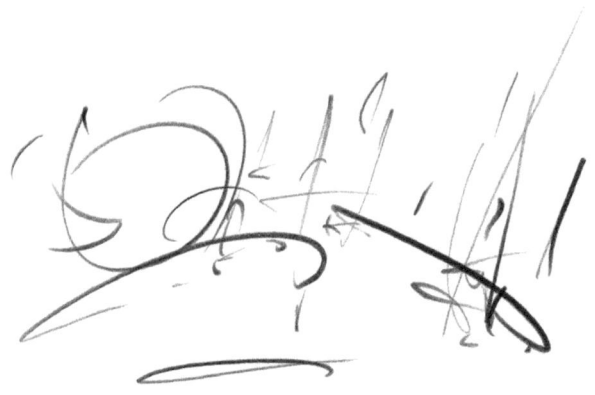

essence. We go from a state of contracted awareness to the true state of unlimited being, transcending space and time. By becoming free from ourselves, we will likewise become filled with the fullness of divine being. In the words of the Japanese Zen Master Dogen Zenji from the thirteenth century:

Truly understanding the true Self means forgetting yourself; forgetting yourself means enlightenment.

The great masters of all religious traditions have time and again pointed out the fact that we must become spiritually empty. Every form of identification and attachment to the transient world of the senses must inevitably lead to suffering. Whatever we may achieve in our lives, be it riches, success or esteem, in the end none of these can bring us lasting contentedness. We remain inwardly unfulfilled and can find no inner peace.

Only by turning inwards to the true source of all happiness will we experience the peace of our true Self. Yet as long as we continue to seek externally in the hope of finding true happiness, our lives will end in discontentment and disappointment. Whichever way we look at it, there is no other way than the way of inner detachment from everything. Whichever worldview we may adhere to, ultimately this will not exempt us from going this path.

Chapter 3

The Directness of Zen

Limited perspective

We humans are generally inclined to fool ourselves by searching for a short cut – a religion that will console us. We are inclined to believe in an ideal world, matching our own wishful thinking, in which each thing finds its correct place, and we cling to a notion of God that is not consistent with reality.

Indeed, everything our discriminating, dualistic thinking can achieve is inevitably limited, and is therefore only ever of superficial and temporal value. The same goes for all the various philosophies and religions. In all that they say, and regardless of how convincing it may sound, they are all just very limited perspectives of the inexpressible truth, but never the truth itself. On this subject there is an old Indian tale:

Five blind men meet an elephant driver seated on an elephant's back. They ask him, "We are blind and have never seen what an elephant looks like.?"

"As you wish," says the elephant driver. The first man feels the trunk and exclaims, "Well I never! The elephant looks like a thick hose!"

The second touches the elephant's ear and declares, "You are wrong, the elephant looks like a big fan!"

The third grasps hold of the tail and says: "No, the elephant looks like a thin rope!"

The fourth grasps the leg and proclaims: "Totally wrong, the elephant looks like a tree stump!"

Finally, the fifth touches the elephant's belly and says, "You are all wrong. The elephant looks like a huge barrel!"

Upon hearing this, the elephant driver says, "None of you is right. Each of you has grasped only a part of the whole but none of you has discerned what the elephant really looks like."

This is how we should understand all assertions on the inexpressible reality by the various religions and philosophies. Only when we ourselves dive directly into the ocean of wisdom, into the boundless ocean of the One Mind, will we come to know the truth. That is why Zen does not offer any philosophical explanations. Zen says: "If you want to know how tea tastes – drink it! Do you want to know how an apple tastes? Then take a bite of the apple! Then you know: that's how it tastes." That is pure Zen.

Zen is always immediate and direct. With the greatest emphasis, it constantly points to your own heart without becoming caught in the tangle of conventions and concepts. It is free, and without this freedom it loses its spontaneity and freshness, ending up as just a dead, empty shell, devoid of all life.

Impermanence

Zen always points to the pure naked truth. It wastes no time with external aesthetic chitchat or mind-bending speculation.

The absolute reality that lies beyond all that changes or can be named will only reveal itself when we are truly prepared to leave everything far behind us that sense and reason can comprehend.

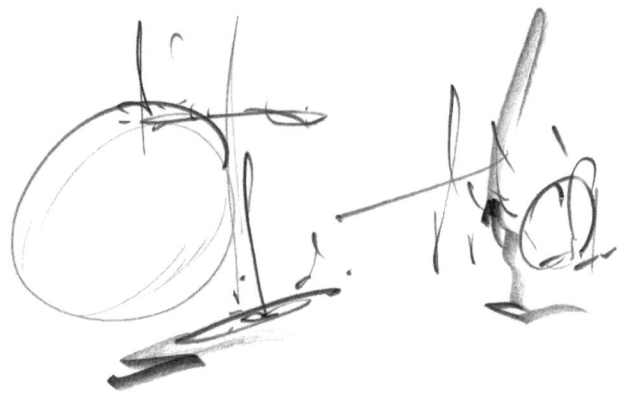

However, as long as we are not prepared to take this decisive step, we live in a state of indifferent non-awareness and mindless routine. We are bound through ourselves and thus remain trapped in our delusion of a stable and ideal world. This state remains until the painful experience of suffering or disappointment finally achieves its purpose and awakens in us the desire for liberation. This is the moment when we recognise that we have been clinging to an illusion. We must go the redemptive way to liberation. In the words of Zen Master Yung-chia from the eighth century:

> The matter of life and death is immense and impermanence swiftly grasps hold. How can you waste your time with trivialities?

Each individual moment we experience is a divine gift and a unique opportunity for realisation, for no one knows whether they will be able to take another breath. The death-bringing demon of impermanence can arrive in an instant and destroy all our hopes.

Whether we believe in Samsara, the cycle of birth and death or not – we are in its midst.

Whether we believe in Karma, the law of cause and effect or not – we are ruled by it.

Whether we are prepared to devote ourselves to spiritual practice or not – death will certainly come to us regardless of whether we are now ready for it.

Therefore, we should recognise how absolutely necessary it is that we immerse ourselves in the spiritual way right now. If not, our death will be no more than the pitiful conclusion to a pointlessly wasted life. This is why Zen Master Lin-chi (ninth century) gives us the admonishing words:

> There is no time to lose. Do not beguile yourselves into great confusion by compulsively rummaging about in the external world instead of seeking within yourselves.

And Zen Master Pai-chang from the ninth century gives us this good piece of advice:

> If you are afraid that at the moment of death you will turn mad with fear and not be able to reach freedom, you should first of all be free in this instant, right now. Then everything will be alright.

Chapter 4

The Action of the One Mind

Being touched by the Eternal

In Zen, completely letting go means detaching yourself from autonomous compulsive thinking, without wishing to forcefully suppress or stop the thinking, and thus it means forgetting yourself and all things. Zen often calls this "being-without-thinking" or "non-thought," known in Chinese as "Wu-nien".

Yet this should by no means be interpreted in a psychological way. Instead, it takes place on a spiritual level where there are no longer any traces of conceptual, analytical thinking. It is that level on which all human activity withdraws in favour of the action of absolute reality.

However, this action of the One Mind cannot be forced by any artificial meditation technique. The mystical experience of being touched and fulfilled by the Divine is always beyond a person's realm of control and cannot be brought about at a wish. Whoever believes he need only apply some spiritual practice or other and will thus automatically achieve the goal of his spiritual striving is greatly deceived. As authorities on the spiritual path, the great enlightened mystics have constantly pointed out this error of "spiritual materialism".

All sacred writings proclaim that enlightenment can only be brought about by the action of the One Mind. So too in the sacred Indian writings of the Upanishads we read:

> Only the one whom He chooses can recognise Him, the Atman manifests its essence to this chosen one.

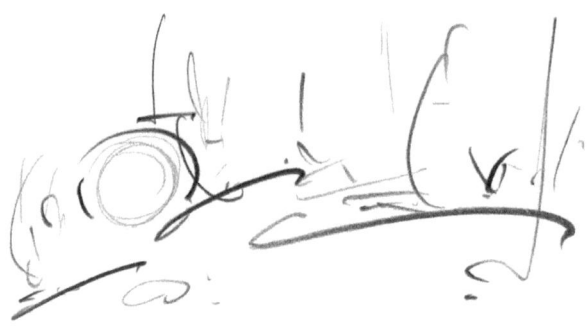

Now one might start to ask, "Is the Universal Mind biased, giving its grace to one person but excluding another? And anyway, why should I make such an effort on the spiritual path when everything just depends on the whim of divine grace?"

When most people think of divine grace, they imagine a personal being with human qualities. Others who believe in an impersonal ultimate reality will ask themselves how – in the language of Buddhism – the "impersonal void" could bestow grace. Indeed, many people imagine attributeless, ultimate reality as a lifeless abstraction, like a creative mechanism, similar to an automated machine.

Abandonment to the Eternal

In truth, however, the One Mind is absolute awareness. It is absolute Beingness – beyond all personal and impersonal attributes – and is thus "transpersonal". Since it is free of all limitations of space and time, it cannot be grasped by a human consciousness limited in space and time.

Yet our trusting in our limited consciousness, bound in space and time, is the reason why grace cannot act within us. By upholding our ego-delusion we hinder ourselves from becoming empty to receive the fullness of divine being, and thus we hinder the action of the One Mind.

However, the more we are prepared to surrender ourselves to the Absolute, the more we will be granted grace as the action of the great Essence beyond space and time. And the more it acts in us, the more we are capable of ever greater and more steadfast self-surrender.

Surrendering ourselves to the Eternal means opening ourselves and "becoming transparent to the transcendental". It means letting go and becoming empty in the form of opening up to something

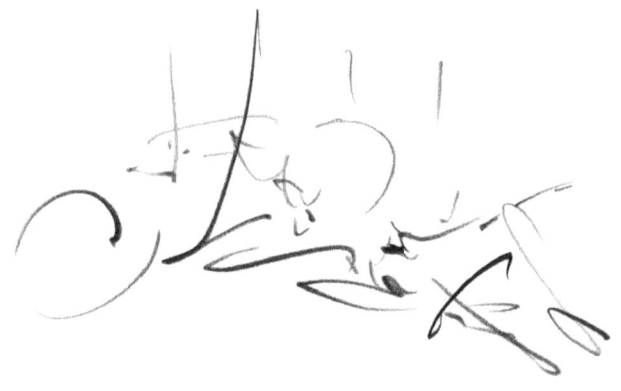

completely different and thus becoming filled by it. Whoever, out of love of the Eternal, lets go of this small life in space and time, likewise opens themselves to the great life beyond space and time that is waiting for them. In this inner detachment, the reality of our true Self, which exists concealed within us in our innermost being then becomes a vivacious, inner experience. In the words of Meister Eckhart from the fourteenth century:

> Unmoving detachment leads a person into the Great Equality with God. It draws a person into purity and simplicity, and from simplicity into immutability.
>
> This engenders an equality between a person and God. Yet this equality must be borne of grace, for grace draws a person forth from all temporal things.

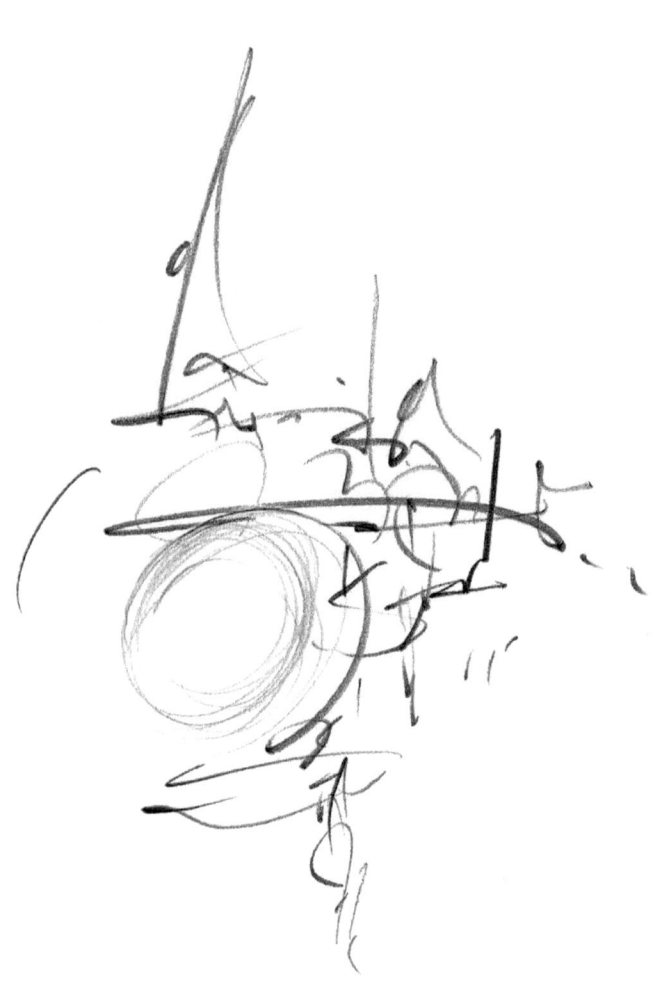

Chapter 5

Relinquishing all Delusions

No teachings

There is no doctrine to study. This is the essential prerequisite for understanding the truth of Zen. All artificial methods and doctrines are in the eyes of Zen no more than hocus-pocus – puffs of air in empty space. There is nothing to be attained and there is no sacred truth to be fulfilled, for even the slightest notion that something can be attained is once again delusion.

As long as we still trust in external teachings and borrowed doctrines we remain far away from the reality of our true being. We are bound by the delusions of our discriminating, conceptual thinking and have confined ourselves.

Each defined teaching is a danger for the free mind. These teachings are dangerous when they become dogmas and enchain the mind. Furthermore, our preoccupation with all sorts of teachings and artificial methods only leads to us wasting our precious time and squandering our spiritual energy.

There is nothing to learn and nothing to gain. This is a basic principle of Zen. Whoever believes there is something to seek on the Zen way is like a blind man in a dark room searching for a black cat that does not exist. The Chinese masters of old constantly referred with utmost emphasis to the fact that, on the Zen way, there is nothing to be gained. Zen Master Huang-po thus says:

> The many methods that are meant to work against the many forms of illusion are no more than sayings, which are there to draw in people to the gates of liberation. In reality, none of them has any real substance. Relinquishing everything is the highest truth. Whoever does this is a buddha. But relinquishing all deceptions leaves no teaching behind that one can rely on.

Thus, true learning in the spirit of Zen is learning that there is nothing to learn and nothing to seek. For where nothing is sought, the Unborn Mind is present. It is also constantly present whilst we are seeking it. Yet precisely due to our seeking and brooding, we cover it with the dark clouds of our discriminating ignorance.

Boundless liberation

As long as we still seek and are prey to the erroneous assumption of there being something to find, be it as tiny as a speck of dust, we have already fallen into the realm of duality. We have fallen into the realm of affirmation and negation, of distinguishing between right and wrong, and we entangle ourselves ever more in Samsara, the cycle of birth and death.

The dualistic state of mind is the true cause of our attachment to Samsara. It spawns all habitual thoughts and actions, and keeps all deceptive notions alive. However, the radiating, untarnished One Mind will only reveal itself when the mind has been purified of the creeping tangle of discriminating thinking.

In this boundless liberation nothing remains to be done. There is no longer any special religious practice to be performed. There is nothing more we could use to lean on for the simple reason that we no longer need anything to lean on – we no longer need crutches.

"Rise, take up thy bed and walk!" says Jesus to the lame man. The lame man is the one who has lost his reality and has forgotten who he is. Due to his earth-binding identification with temporal things he cannot free himself from the attractions of the world. He lies on the earth and cannot rise. Then he hears the call: "Rise, take up thy bed and walk!"

This is the relinquishment of all delusions. This is total liberation. It is how we rise above all our conditionings and thus above the identification with the entwined memories of our dead past.

Once we have reached this clarity and have the courage to leave everything as it is, the reality of what we really are will shine forth. We were crippled and now we can walk again. We were blind and now our eyes have been opened. We will transcend the whole universe and be free from birth and death.

Chapter 6

The Wisdom of Letting Go

Non-action

The path of Zen is above all about liberating ourselves from our false perspectives. Thus, it would be reasonable for us to think: "Alright, I shall make an effort to let go."

However, this type of forced letting go is not the true letting go in the spirit of Zen for it does not correspond to the attitude of mind of wu-wei, "non-action," and wu-nien, "non-thinking". Rather, it is just the desire to let go and thus an activity of the ego. Furthermore, this desire causes inner tension, for tension is always suppressed desire.

Therefore, you cannot dissolve your attachment by "doing" its opposite of letting go, since all opposites such as: being and nonbeing, life and death and right and wrong belong to the dualistic realm of ignorance.

To elucidate this, let us now hear about the encounter of a Zen monk with the Chinese Zen Master Joshu in the ninth century.

A monk comes to Zen Master Joshu and says,

"Look master, I have let go of everything. What do you say to that?" To further clarify his point he waggles demonstratively with his wide sleeves. The aged Master Joshu looks at the monk with a bored expression and says, "Well then throw it away!" The monk is visibly confused by Joshu's answer and thinks that old Joshu could not have understood him due to his old age, so he says, "But master, I just told you that I have let go of everything. What is left for me to throw away?" To this Joshu replies, "Well, if that is the case, you will just have to keep on carrying it!"

This answer by one of the most important masters in the history of Zen has the sharpness of a samurai sword but the monk was clinging too much to his notion of having let go. Therefore, Joshu's blow with the sword was sadly unable to help him reach an insight and awaken him to the true life.

In order to achieve a letting go in terms of Zen we must resolutely cut off all attachments. Let everything go, whatever it may be. In the language of Zen "MU" – "Nothing!" This MU is the nothingness in terms of space and time and thus the nothingness in terms of the entire contents of the consciousness. This MU is

Now – and this Now is eternity. You must recognise this and completely immerse yourself in it! Then, your mind will become completely free, even when it is bound within the confines of life and death. In the words of the Upanishads, the holy Indian scriptures:

Whoever perceives the eternal truth,
sees neither death, nor illness nor suffering,
in all things he sees but one: the true Self,
and everything is his own.

The laughing Buddha

In this awareness state of wonderful clarity we no longer become embroiled in empty fantasies and the vanities of material passions. Free from attachments to the world of the senses, nothing can deceive us any longer. We live unbound in the midst of the world and pass through birth and death in complete freedom. We come and go as we please and are completely free and independent. In Chinese Zen painting we often encounter "Hotei," known in Zen as the "laughing buddha". Hotei is usually depicted as a small, bald, fat man with a large sack slung over his shoulder and a broad smile covering his whole face. In Zen, this laughing buddha represents the one who is totally liberated, having broken through all boundaries and transcended the world.

Hotei lived in the eighth century during the Tang dynasty, the golden age of Zen Buddhism in China. He was a Zen master of highest spiritual fulfilment, yet he had no desire whatsoever to live in a monastery and instruct disciples. Instead, he wandered through the villages with a sack over his shoulder and handed out sweets to the children.

Hotei lived the free life of a Zen tramp, unattached and independent. Like the wind in the trees and the moon on the water he lived his life in total freedom and harmony with the all-embracing whole.

One day Hotei met a Zen monk who asked him, "What is the secret of Zen?" Hotei's silent response was to let the sack he was carrying on his back fall to the ground and to spread out his arms. "Then tell me," asked the monk, "what is the essence of Zen realisation?" The "laughing buddha" immediately grabbed his sack, slung it over his shoulder, and continued on his way laughing loudly and without looking back.

Freedom and cheerfulness of mind is the natural state of our true being. Simply free your mind of everything, whatever it may be. If we just take each situation as it arises, we will be in complete harmony with everything.

Chapter 7

The Original Condition of the Mind

All-embracing wholeness

The original condition of our mind is the reality behind all experiences. It is the One Mind, beside which nothing else exists, and which remains completely untouched by all forms of change and by death. In their essence, the One Mind and your own mind are one and the same reality. Therefore, perceiving the nature of your own mind means perceiving the nature of the all-embracing entirety of being.

The One Mind is like the screen behind all pictures, movements, colours, and forms of a motion picture. When, in the experience of mystical death, you are united with this impartial observer of all experiences, you experience the original state of the mind. The boundless expanse of the One Mind reveals itself in this experience of emptiness, as vast and open as the sky. The mind, which was confined within a self-made boundary, with which it then identified itself, now expands into endlessness and experiences itself as unborn and deathless. However, this liberation of the mind is not something we can do deliberately. Yet when we immerse ourselves in the immediate moment of Now, we reach a state of forgetting ourselves and all things. This means we are beyond space and time – beyond the notion of past and future, which are no more than empty thoughts.

Our experience of past, present, and future is as fleeting as a leaf, blown past the window of our consciousness by the autumn wind. Space and time form the basis for our experience of the world, yet a single instant in the immediate presence of pure awareness and we are in absolute "now," and the spectre of our "space-time illusion" dissolves away. Here, there is no I and no you, no coming and no going. Here, there is only "Now". This Now has no "before" and no "after," and thus it is eternity. It is the reality of divine being of which Meister Eckhart says, "God is absolute 'Now.'"

We need not seek it anywhere; we need not go anywhere. Where would we seek the reality of our true being that we ourselves are and that neither begins with birth nor ends with death? Where would we find the "divine light that shines in the darkness," to use the words of the prologue to the Gospel of John – where would we find it apart from within ourselves?

Yet one thought and then another thought, and the myriad feelings and notions have already begun to form. All this obscures the true condition of the mind, with the result that we cannot recognise the divine light that shines in the darkness.

The light of our true being

We can never perceive this light, our true being, by means of the intellect's capacity of perception. It would be just like wanting to find a candle, burning on a large open space in bright sunshine. It must be completely dark. "MU" – nothing! Non-desire, non-thinking – finally having the courage to leave everything just as it is. This is the great faith that we must reach.

If we really wish to achieve liberation we must free ourselves of every attachment. When life comes and reveals itself to us, we accept it just as it is. When death comes, we accept death. Then everything is very simple. This life and this death are Buddha's life and death. Let everything go, whatever it may be – "MU" – nothing! MU is nothingness with respect to coming and going in space and time. Thus it is the nothingness with respect to all contents of the consciousness, whatever they may be.

It is most important to awaken this great faith within ourselves. This takes place when, instead of relying on ourselves, on our intellectual capabilities, we abide in wu-nien, in "Non-thinking". Through this we become empty for the fullness of divine being, so that Tao can work in us and through us. In the words of Meister Eckhart: God acts and I become.

We cannot force anything, for the simple reason that there is nothing to achieve. As soon as we believe there is something to achieve, some goal to reach, we find ourselves in the hell of the demons of discriminating thought.

Yet these demons are none other than our own

projections, for we are chasing after a wishful notion that only exists in our head. Yet "Now," everything is here! We lack nothing at all, not the slightest thing. We are absolute being, boundless awareness, and infinite bliss, and all else is just bubbles, dreams and shadows, devoid of all reality.

Chapter 8

Non-Discriminating Clarity

Embracing and rejecting

Everywhere, wherever it may be, the reality we are seeking is present. "Everything is filled with the fullness of God." The glory of divine being reveals itself in everything. If we do not find it "Now-Here" in the midst of daily life, we will find it neither in a Buddhist temple, nor in a church nor in any other "holy" place. Then it is just another illusion created by our conditioned, discriminating thinking, and we only end up in fooling ourselves. That is why Zen Master Lin-chi says:

> While you love what is holy and loathe what is common, you are still bobbing up and down in the sea of ignorance.

You must rise above both of these – the profane and the sacred! Free yourself of all your dualistic notions. This is true non-discrimination: neither accepting nor rejecting. That is why it is said in Zen:

"You have yet to take leave of the family!" In other words, you have still not left behind your conditionings, that is: the ways in which you think and act. You continue to be a prisoner of all your stencils and fixations, and you are yet to abide in the cloudless clarity of the mind.

Only when we are free of wanting and hating, that

is to say, of accepting and rejecting, will the highest truth reveal itself clearly and infinitely. It reveals itself when we no longer take the option to make preferences. Yin and Yang belong together and complement one another. We cannot have one without the other. It would be just like wanting to have an electric current with no minus pole, just the plus pole. Or like wanting the sun to shine every day and never have rain again. Everything is the one reality; be it a pretty butterfly, be it a beautiful flower, or be it a stinking dung heap. To this, the following Zen-encounter:

A Zen student asked the Chinese Zen Master Yun-men from the tenth century: "Who is the buddha of all buddhas of the past, present, and future?" The master replied, "A stick covered in excrement."

Why differentiate? Everything is one, for everything is an all-encompassing whole, containing everything within itself – there is nothing we can remove. Even when you split an atom in a laboratory, this splitting merely transforms it into another form of energy. We cannot destroy anything, dissolve it, or make it disappear. Things can only be transformed, for they are bound by the universal law of transformation.

Harmonic transformation

The harmonic transformation of the Tao reveals itself in everything. It is the creative first principle from out of which all things are born, sustained and once again dissolved in never ending plenitude. Thus it is the original principle of all being – beginningless and eternal. It is the Absolute, the highest transcendence, the one reality, existing of itself, from which the universe originates.

Zen is about being in harmony with this all-embracing motion of the One. When we flow with it,

with the eternal transformation of the Tao, we do not oppose it and thus we are in unison with reality. Therefore, make no distinction, for everything is good just as it is. Of course, it is not easy to accept this truth, but in the end we have no alternative but to accept it – not in pessimistic resignation, but through insight. We cannot change the world – but we can change ourselves. We can experience the world as a wonderful paradise, or we can experience it as hell – it is all up to us. To illustrate this, let us hear about the encounter between Zen Master Hakuin from the eighteenth century and a samurai:

A samurai comes to Zen Master Hakuin and says: "The question of heaven and hell has been bothering me for a long time. Therefore, I would like to ask you: is there really such a thing as paradise and hell?"

Hakuin says, "Who are you to just come along and ask me such a stupid question?"

"Can't you see? I'm a samurai of the Imperial Guard!" replies the samurai, full of pride.

Hakuin starts to laugh and says, "Impossible, our emperor would never engage such a wretched looking character as you. You look like a miserable beggar to me."

Filled with rage, the samurai reaches for his sword and wrenches it out.

Hakuin raises his hand and says, "The gates to hell have just opened."

As if struck by lightning, the samurai stops, puts his sword away, and bows to Hakuin.

And Hakuin says, "The gates to paradise have just opened."

We alone project this entire theatre-world, this entire dream world, just as we perceive it. All of it is nothing more than unrestrained projections of our consciousness.

Therefore, it is very important that we acquire constant awareness of mind and non-discriminating clarity in the midst of daily life. This means that during all activities, wherever we may be, we see through the deceptive nature of all phenomena so that we recognise all phenomena as being empty.

When we recognise all phenomena as being empty, we can reside in the ordinary world every day and nevertheless be completely independent. When we have achieved this realisation, we are free like the wind in the trees and the birds in the sky. As the master of each situation, we become one with all the manifold circumstances. We are vast and open like boundless space, without limits or bounds and we live in the midst of the world in complete freedom.

Chapter 9

Neither Being nor Non-Being

Opposites

Everything is the One Mind, beside which nothing else exists. It is pure being in itself, independent of everything that has gone before, and thus its essence emanates from out of itself. As the sole reality it is the Absolute, the Suchness of all things. Since the One Mind is beyond all opposites, it is neither this nor that, for it does not belong to that category of things that exist or do not exist. Due to its inherent inexpressibility it is not possible for us to define it more closely.

Western philosophy says, "To be or not to be, that is the question!" But the non-dualistic viewpoint of Zen is completely the opposite. And so we read in the Pi-yen-lu, the Blue Cliff Record, one of the fundamental Zen texts from the twelfth century:

> Whoever reflects upon being or non-being loses life and limb!

When we say that the One Mind is neither being nor non-being, it means that it is beyond all contraries. Yet as soon as a designation appears, be it just one single thought, a second thought will follow and then we are in the realm of opposites.

Zen Master Tokusan from the ninth century had a very particular way of demonstrating this to his students:

> Once, Zen Master Tokusan came into the monks hall, raised his staff and said, "If you have any word to say, I will give you thirty blows with my staff.
> Yet should you have no word to say, you will also receive thirty blows all over your skull."

The moment something becomes conceptually fixed, its opposite will instantly arise of its own accord. That is why Lao-tse, the founding father of Taoism, says in the sixth century B.C.:

> When everyone knows: beauty is beautiful,
> then ugliness is already there.
> When everyone knows: goodness is good,
> then evil is already there.

Good and bad, yes and no, right and wrong are all manifestations of discriminating conceptual thought. This discriminating intellect-consciousness forms the basis of our experiences. It projects all sorts of notions and defines reality based on relative opposites.

Yet behind this entire deception of a projecting consciousness lies our true Self. It is like a clear mirror, on whose surface all projections take place. However, the self remains completely untouched, regardless of what happens. Nevertheless, most people in their conditioned worldview are so identified with their projecting consciousness that they regard themselves as being the thinker of their thoughts. But this is a totally wrong way of viewing things since the thinker is no more than the sum of the thoughts.

There is no individual self-existing thinker who is separate from the process of thinking, however much we may still believe we are a static, continuous entity. Essentially, there is nothing more than an un-interrupted, complex succession of thoughts.

This sum of rapid, sequential thoughts arouses in us the deceptive impression of an individual consciousness that acts within the illusion of space and time. Since this conditioned, limited consciousness in space and time erroneously believes it is something that lies beyond the thoughts, beyond the perceptions, it regards itself as being the centre of this whole business. And exactly that is the constant process of formation and perpetuation of the ego-delusion.

Liberation from concepts

By not recognising the emptiness of all phenomena we identify with our old modes of thought and then believe, "this is the world and this is my personality". All our memories, this whole sum of experiences which we have identified with from the first day of our childhood onwards make up our assumed individuality. As it hardens into the armour of the ego, this habitual, identifying way of viewing the world forms the illusion of an independent, self-existing personality. It believes it is separate from everything it perceives and experiences.

Yet when we break through this whole delusion, we come closer and closer to an inner detachment from all our false perspectives, since the notion of a personal self is our real bond. Therefore, our liberation can only happen when we let go of the delusion of an independent personality.

If we really want to put an end to our enslavement in the cycle of birth and death, there is no other way than

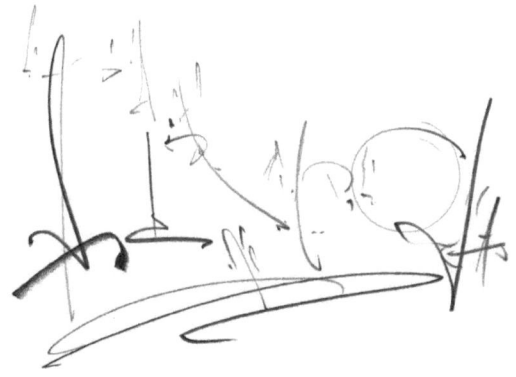

to let go of all our concepts. We must rid ourselves of everything we have ever upheld in our minds and deemed important, for: "Nothing is important in the face of the presence of death!" This is why Zen Master Yun-men says in the tenth century:

Time waits for no one: one day your dying gaze will turn to the ground and then, what will you do then? Do not wave your arms and legs around in despair like a crab thrown into hot water!

This will definitely not be the place for big words from you big mouths!

"True words are not pleasant, pleasant words are not true," says the Taoist sage Lao-tse. The deeper a statement is, and the more directly it touches the heart of the matter, the less uplifting are its words as seen from a normal viewpoint. They always tear the foundation of our ego stability from under our feet, and everything that gives us ostensible security in this space-time dimension of samsaric delusion dissolves away.

Yet when we recognise – when we really understand that our personality has no real existence anyway and that it is no more than an illusion – we will reach the point where we are ready to inwardly let go of everything.

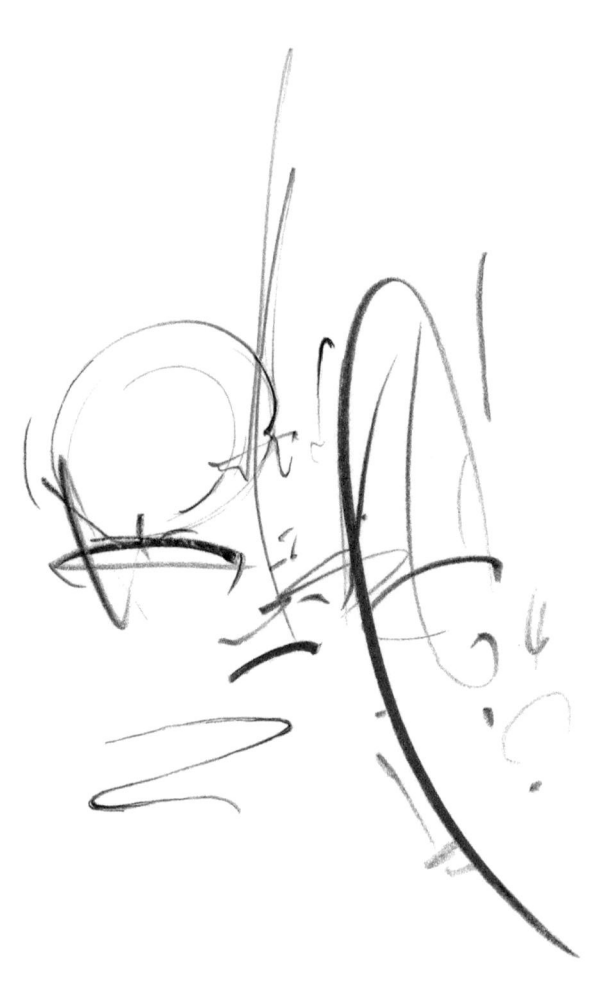

Chapter 10

Beyond Life and Death

Fear of death

Whoever clings to his mundane life at the moment of death only shows that he is still dominated by his small "ego-self". Since life within the bounds of space and time constitutes the only tangible reality of being for him, he clings tightly to the personal ego, which he continues to equate with his own life. This clasping is the real cause of his fear of death.

Fear of death has its roots in the illusion of a mortal self, clinging with all its might to the delusion of a personality, existing in its own right. Yet whoever in the enlightenment experience has witnessed his immortal self and thus the unreality of that grasping, mortal "pseudo-ego," no longer clings to life nor does he fear death. He has reached a spiritual state "beyond life and death".

For this reason, the Japanese Zen Master Uesugi Kenshin from the sixteenth century tells us:

Those who overly cling to life will die, and

those who accept death will live. It is the inner not the outer that counts. Look within and you will experience that something lives within you that is beyond birth and death and can neither drown in water nor burn in fire. I myself have reached this insight and so I know what I am talking about.

Such a resolute concentration on death trained the Zen students of former times to a state of mind of absolute steadfastness. The Zen of the ancient masters

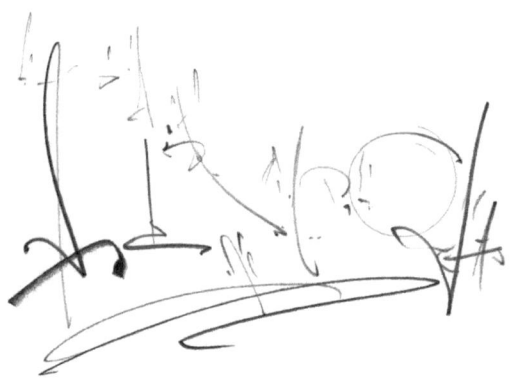

was a matter of life and death, and the encounter between master and student was always of great earnestness, as in the following story:

One day, the great Chinese Zen Master Ma-tsu from the eighth century was lying across a cart track. He stretched his limbs and rested. A monk came along from his work in the fields with a wheelbarrow and asked him to pull in his legs so that he could continue his way.

"Let lie, what lies," said Ma-tsu.

"And let roll what rolls," answered the monk, pushing the wheelbarrow over the master's legs. Later that evening when all were gathered in the great hall, Ma-tsu seized a huge axe and roared, "Let him who drove over my legs this afternoon come forward!" Without hesitation, the monk approached, bowed, and held out his neck for the master. Ma-tsu nodded approvingly and set the axe aside.

Liberation from the ego-delusion

The remarkable self-confidence and fearlessness the monk had attained through his Zen training demonstrated to Ma-tsu that his student's state of mind was beyond life and death.

Achieving such a holistic state of awareness requires the death of a person's ego. In this process he must break through the boundaries of his consciousness, limited by his ignorance. Yet since there is no "individual self," existing of its own accord, this death of the ego can only mean the death of all identifications and attachments causing the ego-delusion. In the words of Zen Master Yang-shan from the ninth century:

> You should turn your attention inwards. For longer than you can remember you have turned to darkness away from the light, and thus the roots of your ego-clinging thoughts go deep and are hard to pull out.

Without eradication, that is: without the death of the fearful attachment to the delusion of an ego, we remain chained to "Samsara," the cycle of birth and death. This cycle takes place under the remorseless law of "Karma," namely, the retribution of all deeds performed in this external world of phenomena.

Karma and reincarnation are tightly interwoven with the ego-delusion, for as long as "ego-focussing" exists, caused by the ignorance of our true innate nature, we continue to take the illusion of an apparent multitudinous world to be real.

This causes us to commit all sorts of deeds out of

desire, rejection and spiritual blindness, thus entangling ourselves all the more in the creeping tangle of our attachments, brought about by our identifications. We have no possibility of escape from this, except through the experience of mystical death, in which the ego-delusion is radically obliterated.

Chapter 11

Great Liberation

Mystical death

True spiritual practice is a matter of life and death, which ultimately means the death of the ego. We will only perceive the true nature of our being when we radically turn inwards, by dying into our deepest original essence. Only when we have been renewed through the baptism of mystical death can we experience the fullness of divine life. The Christian mystic Meister Eckhart (fourteenth century) tells us this too:

He who beholds God perceives nothing as God. If you wish to be united with God, you should wholly sink away from your you-ness and dissolve into His His-ness, and your 'yours' and His 'His' should become so completely one 'Mine' that with Him you eternally perceive His unbecome Is-ness and His nameless Nothing-ness.

In the words of the Chinese Zen Master Ta-hui from the twelfth century:

> Die completely and utterly, then return to life
> – nothing can deceive you anymore.

This mystical dying is the "great liberation" and is known in Zen as "the great death". The great death and the great liberation are one and the same. The sole requirement for experiencing this is that we let go of everything this instant, whatever it may be, and thus achieve a state in which we forget ourselves and all things.

In this state of letting go, our true being reveals itself to us. Completely letting go and dissolving into the fullness of divine being is "one" experience and both take place in the same instant. In this experience of mystical death we are transformed into the radiating light of the Mind and we are filled with great clarity and indescribable peace.

This is great liberation. The bonds of the ego-delusion are broken, and from now on we live a life in complete freedom. To elucidate this, let us now hear the old Indian tale of the king and his parrot:

The king and his parrot

A long time ago there was once a parrot, which lived with many other parrots in a tree in the jungle. They were all very happy and contented and ate from the wonderful jungle fruits.

But one day, the king's hunters came along and caught the parrot in a net. And since it was a beautiful parrot with bright shiny feathers in green, blue, red and yellow, the king said:

"This is now my palace-parrot." And he commanded his goldsmiths to build a great cage of pure gold. The small hatchway for entering the cage was covered with diamonds, and the bowls for eating and drinking were fitted with rubies and emeralds. It was given the best food a parrot could ever dream of. Yet the parrot was always very sad since it had indeed lost its freedom and was trapped.

One day, the king said to him, "Listen here, parrot, I am going on a great journey – and guess where – right to the place where you lived in the jungle. And I'll be passing the tree where all your friends live. If you want, I can pass on a message from you. Should I say hello from you? Or anything else?"

The parrot replied: "Tell them the truth, just as it is.

Tell them that I live here in your palace in a cage."

"Yes, that you are here in a wonderful golden cage," said the king, "and that you are fine and happy."

"That is not the truth! You know the truth. I have everything I need to eat and drink ... I have a golden cage with jewels and all the other fancy things. But I

miss my freedom. I wish to be free and don't know what to do. Tell my friends exactly that. And ask them what they advise me to do to feel free and happy again."

The next morning the king departed with his entourage. On arriving at the said tree he ordered them to stop. The parrots in the tree quickly sought safety on seeing the king and his men arrive. The king called up to them, "There's no need to be afraid. I come from your friend, who now lives with me in the palace, and I have a message for you!"

They flew a little nearer and called out:" Well – what is it, what is it?"

"I have been asked to tell you that he lives with me in the palace in a wonderful, big cage made of pure gold, covered with jewels, rubies and emeralds – and he has the finest food!"

"Well," said the parrots, "is that everything?"

"Hmmm.... no," said the king, avoiding an answer.

"Come on, tell us!"

"He said he is very unhappy and suffers because he is captive, and he doesn't know what to do to feel free and happy again."

"Oh-oh, how awful," the parrots wailed and drooped their heads. "Our poor friend!" Each of them folded its wings before its chest, and then all of a sudden, one of them rolled its eyes and fell from the tree. After a while, another one fell and then another and then another. And then suddenly they had all fallen from the tree and stirred no more.

"Oh," moaned the king, "this is terrible, how could it happen? They are all dead! Dead parrots everywhere! Was it such a shock for them to hear that their friend sits in a wonderful golden cage in my palace and has everything you could dream of and is still unhappy?

This is terrible. The poor things. – I have no idea how I'm going to tell this to my parrot."

When the king had more or less recovered from his shock he continued his journey. Finally, he returned to the palace with his men. On entering the room, the parrot was already waiting impatiently in its cage. He held his head askew and asked: "Well, what happened? Did you meet my friends?"

"Well…," said the king, evading an answer.

"And you passed on my message to them?"

"Yes, yes."

"So what did they say then?"

"Hmmm, well nothing in fact," replied the king.

"Why not? They must have said something!"

"They all fell from the tree."

"What? What do you mean 'fell from the tree'?"

"Well I gave them your message."

"What did you say to them?"

"Just as you said: that you live with me in a golden cage and have everything one could wish for. And that just the same, you are unhappy because you do not know what you can do to feel happy and free again."

"Yes, and then?"

"Then they all fell down and were dead."

"Whaaat? All dead?!" the parrot cried, and clasped

his wings to his chest. He rolled his eyes, started to sway, then fell from his perch. He lay on the floor of his cage and no longer moved.

"Ohh," cried the king, "My parrot! My parrot is dead too ... how terrible, oh how terrible!" He called his servant and said to him, "We must bury my parrot, and since he is the royal parrot we want to give him a worthy burial. Bring a funeral stretcher and place him on a cushion of red satin. Tomorrow we will carry him to his grave."

The following morning the great moment of the funeral ceremony arrived. The priests led the procession in their ceremonial dress, and the musicians of the court orchestra played their funeral music. At the centre of the funeral procession the parrot was carried on top of the stretcher. All the people were sorrowful and lamented, "Oh, the king's parrot is dead, what a shame, how sad."

But suddenly the parrot started to move and sat up. It flapped its wings, and to the surprise of everyone

rose up above the mourners. It flew high over the king's head – circled a couple of times and called, "Thank-you, thank-you my dear king! Thank-you so much for this wonderful message from my friends. They haven't really died. This was just their way of telling me: 'There is only one way to liberation and that is to die out of the cage!'"

Having said this, he rose up high into the air and flew away.

Chapter 12

Zen - The Wisdom of Non-Seeking

Seeking without seeking

The reality we are seeking only reveals itself when we realise that there is nothing to seek. In the words of the Indian sage Ramana Marharshi from the last century:

> The day will come on which you will laugh about your past endeavours. What you will recognise on the day on which you laugh is already "here" and already "now".

In the eyes of Zen, all forms of seeking are nothing more than ignorance. When you do not seek anything you remain detached and relaxed.

We cannot reach our true being, the unborn One Mind, since there is nothing to reach. For this reason, the Chinese Zen Master Fo-yan from the twelfth century says:

When you seek – what is the difference from chasing after sound and form? When you do not seek – then how do you differ from earth, wood and stone?

You must seek without seeking!

In other words, become silent, abide within yourself and thus allow yourself to be found by the all-embracing, omnipresent reality of the One Mind.

Meister Eckhart puts it as follows:

A person need not beg for God's grace. He must only make himself prepared for its action.

We can see this too in the parable of the man standing at the gates of paradise and trying to enter. At first he knocks tentatively on the gates, then after a while a little harder, but nothing happens. Then he pounds with his fists, but without success. Despairingly, he kicks the gates. Then he takes a run-up and runs at the gates, yet they do not open. This continues the whole night until he finally collapses to the ground, exhausted, and realises that all his attempts were in vain. Yet lo and behold: the gates open, but in the opposite direction – namely towards him.

Goal-orientation

All our seeking and our attempts to reach the unreachable do nothing other than to push shut the gates to liberation. "That there is nothing to be reached are not empty words but the highest truth," says Zen Master Huang-po. As evident as these words may sound, only very few people understand them. Although many quickly agree and say, "there is nothing to achieve," intellectually speaking they remain goal-oriented and keep this up, regardless of what they do – even during meditation.

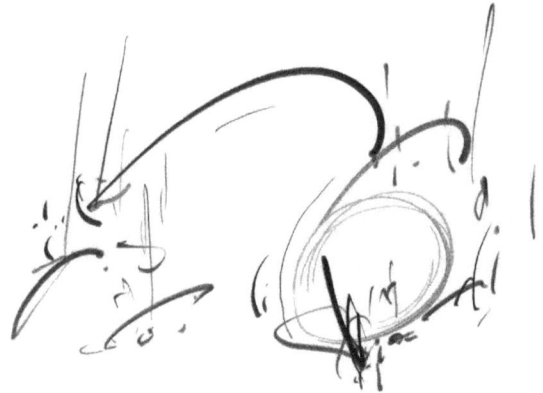

Many truth-seekers struggle this way for years on end, without ever achieving the fruits of their endeavours. Yet for some, the eye of enlightenment only opened when they had abandoned their efforts.

In the ninth century, the aged Chinese Zen monk Hsiang-yen had this experience too:

> After years of fruitlessly struggling for enlightenment, Hsiang-yen gave up his life in the monastery. He withdrew into solitude and lived the life of a recluse in an old, run-down shack. One day, whilst sweeping in front of his shack, a little pebble sprang up and bounced off the bamboo shaft of his broom. The sound it produced quite unexpectedly opened Hsiang-yen's mind and in an instant he achieved enlightenment. Subsequently, he broke out in great laughter. Thereupon he wrote the following enlightenment-gatha:
>
> With one stroke, all previous knowledge is forgotten. No toilsome working on oneself is required to this end. All those who have experienced enlightenment declare this to be the highest truth of all.

The revelation of buddha-nature, our true Self, has been taking place throughout all eternity Now-Here. When we are here, everything is here! In the absolute presence of Now, our original face before our birth reveals itself.

A monk asks Zen Master Tien-lung (ninth century), "Who is buddha?"

Tien-lung says, "You are he."

The monk: "How am I to understand this?"

Tien-lung: "Do you want a handle on your begging bowl?"

Chapter 13

True Zen-Spirit

Wrong meditation practice

Most people practice meditation in order to achieve something. They wish to achieve Buddhahood, that is, enlightenment. They wish to wallow in wonderful, blissful feelings and dwell in silence and peacefulness.

On this, Meister Eckhart says:

> Whoever believes to have more from God through silent immersion, prayer, dulcet feelings, and particular endearment than from standing in front of the hearth or being in the stable, seeks God in particular forms. He grasps at the form but God evades him. Yet only he who seeks God in no form at all will grasp Him as He is unto Himself.

True Zen meditation means being free from all desires – being free from everything, whatever it may be. In Zen, the common term for this is "Mushotoku," which means, "Being without goals and striving for gain".

Just as it is wrong to bathe in wonderful, enrapturing feelings during meditation, it is equally wrong to just sit there, waiting for enlightenment. For how can we ever expect to achieve insight into our true being by just mindlessly sitting around? The Zen monk Ma-tsu in the eighth century had to recognise this too:

At the time when Ma-tsu was still a disciple in the monastery of his Master Nan-yueh, he sat day in, day out for many hours at a time in meditative contemplation. One day, whilst sitting immersed in the monastery courtyard, his master came up to him and asked, "What are you hoping to achieve by sitting absorbed for hours on end?"

Ma-tsu replied, "I wish to gain Buddhahood this way."

Without uttering a word, Master Nan-yueh turned around and went into the garden. After a while he returned with a stone and a roof tile and began to grate the stone against the tile. Young Ma-tsu's sacred peace and tranquillity were shattered by the grinding noise. He strove to ignore the terrible noise but Master Nan-yueh continued unremittingly to grate the stone against the tile. Finally, having put up with the ordeal for several minutes, Ma-tsu could no longer contain himself and called out irascibly, "Master, why are you grinding this stone and the tile together all the time?"

Nan-yueh replied: "I plan to make a wonderful, shining mirror out of the tile."

Totally baffled, Ma-tsu then asked, "But how can you make a mirror by grinding a roof tile?"

To this Master Nan-yueh answered, "And how can anyone reach Buddhahood by just sitting in contemplation?"

In this way, Zen Master Nan-yueh wanted to make it clear to his student, who later went on to become one of the most significant masters in the history of Zen, that Buddhahood – experiencing our true being – cannot be forced by external, artificially imposed practice.

True Zen practice

When we desperately try to reach enlightenment by sitting cross legged for hours on end, we kill the true spirit of Zen.

The ancient Chinese Zen masters called this false form of meditation practice "the ghost cave of the dead void". Zen Master Lin-chi has the following to say about this type of false practice:

> There are the blind bald-headed ones who, after they have stuffed themselves full, practise

meditation for hours on end. They arrest the movement of their thoughts and to prevent them from even forming, they flee the noise of the world and seek quietude. This is a deviant form of Zen. It is the pitfall of the dead void.

Nevertheless, we should not forget that for spiritual practice, mediation is extremely important. Yet this one-sided practice of just sitting in immersion is the

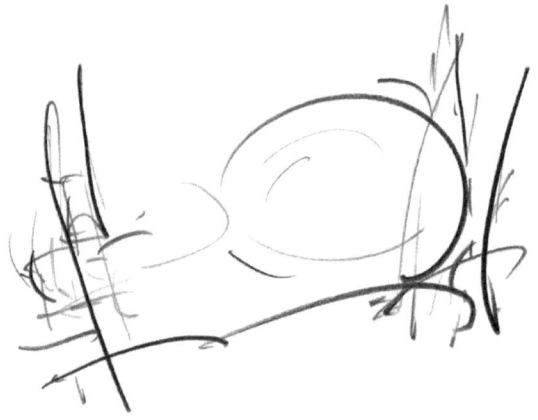

total opposite of the vivacious Zen of the ancient Chinese masters.

Instead, true, original Zen is about retaining a non-attaching mind, everywhere and at all times so that we learn to deal with things in a free, non-identifying way; so that we possess things without them possessing us, and that we act without ego-identification and thus are inwardly free of our actions. This is true life through, out of and in Zen.

True Zen practice is thus not only a particular physical sitting posture but rather an attitude of mind from moment to moment. It is a matter of retaining constant, uninterrupted immersion in our inner ground in all that we do. Whether standing, lying down, sitting, walking, talking, being silent – everywhere and at all times. This is the original, living Zen of the ancient Chinese masters, as expressed in the following mondo – the encounter between master and student:

A student of Zen asked Master Hui-hai, who lived in the eighth century: "Master, what is your way of living Zen – what is the secret of your Zen?"

The master replied, "When I am hungry, I eat, and when I am tired, I sleep."

"Indeed," said the monk, "that's all very well, but all of us do this. What is so special about it?"

"Well," said the master, "when you eat, you have thousands of thoughts and are here and there. And when you sleep, you have many fears and wishes in your dreams. Yet when I eat, I just eat and nothing else. And when I sleep, I sleep and nothing else. That is my Zen."

This is the true spirit of Zen. In this awareness-state of cheerful reflection of the mind, we liberate ourselves from all our attachments and identifications. Everything dissolves away and we abide in the all-embracing wholeness of being – beyond birth and death.

Not that we will never grow any older and die, but it will just happen. The plant grows, the bud opens and blossoms in full splendour and beauty. The flower gives off its wonderful scent, attracting bees and butterflies to take its nectar, and then comes the time when it loses its petals and falls apart. Everything happens quite naturally, just simply in harmonic unison with Tao.

Chapter 14

Cheerfulness of Mind

Here and now is eternity

This instant, right here where you are, the absolute reality of divine being reveals itself. It lies neither in the past nor in the future. Here and Now is eternity – and space and time are nothing other than the result of thinking, with its conditioned perceptions, and thus illusion. So therefore, open yourself completely to this moment of "absolute Now". This is the true way of direct, instantaneous perception of reality, just as it is. Now-here, everything collapses to a single point. In the words of the great Mahamudra Master Saraha in the ninth century:

> Everything that is here is also elsewhere, and what is not here, is nowhere.

Where should we seek for reality when we are already in its midst? Where should we seek the "Pure Land," the Sukhavati-Paradise of boundless light? In the words of Jesus:

The Kingdom of God is within you!

This "within you" is absolute "within-ness" – your centre of being. It is your innermost core, the place and origin of all life. This innermost core is our true being – beyond birth and death and outside of space and time. And thus it can be nothing other than "Now".

The innermost core can never be the past and it can never be the future, for these are all just clouds that pass across the clear light of the mind and have no reality. Behind these, the reality of the One Mind, which is eternal, unborn and indestructible, radiates with undiminished clarity.

Since this is how things are, and since the reality of the One Mind reveals itself as the fundament of all our experiences, it is constantly present. It is directly here – we are right in its midst.

Wherever we go, wherever we dwell – no matter where we are – the unchanging buddha-essence, the original source of the entire universe is present everywhere. So why do we jump restlessly from branch to branch like wild monkeys, grasping at this and that and searching for something that we have in fact never lost?

We can only experience our true being when we

completely immerse ourselves in the original state of
the mind, our true being "Now-Here". Yet the intellect
constantly seeks to set limits and keep everything
under control, since it can keep control of what is
limited and thus avoid opening itself and letting go.
But as long as we cling to our conditioning and the
interwoven memories of our dead past, we will never

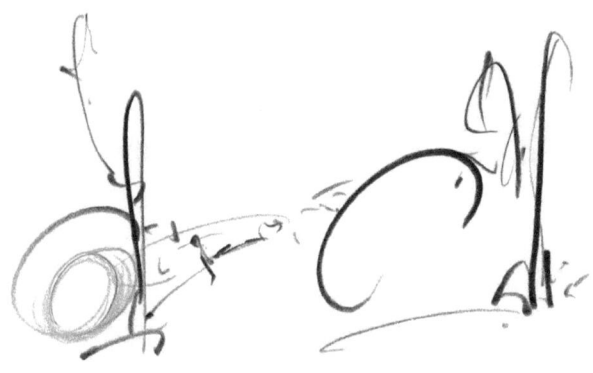

experience the true joy of our divine being. On the
contrary: when divine joy catches sight of us it will
hastily take flight. A humourless person who skulks
through life with a face like a pallbearer can never
become enlightened. Such graveness is a totally
misguided attitude to life. The Vivekachudamani,
one of the fundamental Indian Vedanta scripts from
the ninth century says:

You are Brahman, divine reality. You are pure awareness, the observer behind every experience and your true essence is joy.

But cramped graveness is simply foul and pathological. It is a destructive malady of the soul. A humourless, sombre attitude of mind is always the result of conditioned, ego-centred problem-thinking. Fearfully we peer into the future, and filled with melancholy or a guilty conscience we look back into the past. This state of mind is also the reason for mistrust, jealousy, and envy. It turns the ego into a fortress against everything that surrounds it, with the result that it disquiets the heart and scatters the mind.

The dog in the hall of mirrors

We wear protective armour because we are afraid of being vulnerable and thus we defend ourselves against everything and everyone. Subsequently, we more and more lose the ability to perceive our true being behind all the unrestrained projections of a dualistic consciousness. Eventually, our existence, separated from reality, becomes no more than a tawdry shadow of our true being. As such we become those walking corpses of which Jesus says, "Let the dead bury their own!" Now that we no longer heed the harmonic tone of life, we can only perceive disharmony in the world. Just as a mirror only ever reflects back the face that looks into it, so the external world of phenomena we perceive only ever reflects our individual state of

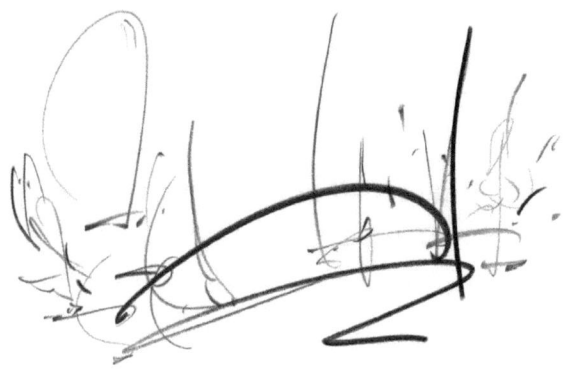

awareness. It is like in the old parable of the dog in the hall of mirrors:

One day, while roaming around, a dog becomes lost in a cave with many passages. He suddenly finds himself in a big hall, surrounded by a thousand mirrors.

Wherever he looks he sees only dogs – nothing but dogs. Frightened and distrustful, he bristles and backs away a few steps. Since the dogs in the thousand mirrors do the same, he begins to growl, snarl, and bare his teeth ferociously. Growing terrified at the huge number of ferocious, snarling dogs he sees all around him, he falls into a state of utter confusion. He begins to run angrily in circles, which, of course, the dogs in the mirrors do as well. This causes him to run faster and faster until all at once, completely exhausted he falls down dead.

Now comes the question: What would have happened had the poor dog just once wagged his tail? And so, stop growling and wag your tails instead! An Indian proverb says,

The smile that you send out will return to you.

The world that we experience is just a reflection of ourselves, and there is no sense in finding fault in a reflection. If we wish to live in a joyful and peaceful world we must begin with ourselves; this is an irrefutable spiritual law.

Chapter 15

Inner Silence in the Face
of the Infinite

Inexpressible secret

The relentless tide of thoughts belongs to human nature. One thought follows the next and they move within their self-made limitations. As a result of this endlessly restless thinking, we can no longer perceive the omnipresent, birthless and deathless reality within ourselves.

For that which exists concealed in our innermost depths lies in silence and tranquillity. In this peace at the depths of divine origin there flows the eternal, inexhaustible original source of all existence. Many words confuse the mind, yet where words are silent, the Eternal begins. For this reason, the Chinese Zen Master Yuan-wu from the twelfth century says:

> Where speaking and thinking no longer have any significance, you will fuse with the Essential, sink into the Eternal, and attain

indwelling wisdom, which knows no attainment.

If we wish to experience the Eternal within us, all thinking, presuming and alluding must cease. Indeed, the more a person is steeped in the fullness of divine being, the harder it becomes for him to express

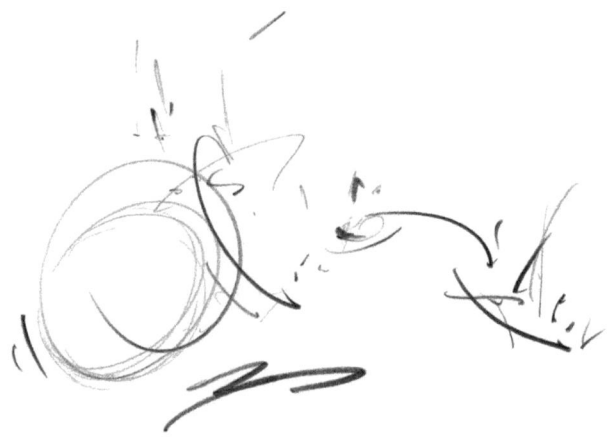

in words the inexpressible mystery of the Eternal. Everything he could say of it would fall short of the mark and not truly express his mystical experience. The Christian mystic Meister Eckhart speaks of this too:

> Everything one can say about God is by no means God at all, for what God really is can a

person only perceive who has been translated into a light which is God Himself.

Whichever names and circumlocutions we may ascribe to the inconceivable and thus unspeakable origin of all being, in the end they are but our own limited conceptions and images of reality, but never absolute reality itself. The divine essence is intangible and indefinable since defining means setting limits. All attempts to force it into conceptual forms are as if one would attempt to capture heaven in a net. For this reason, the ancient Chinese Taoist Master Lao-tse from the sixth century B.C. says:

The speakable Tao is not the eternal Tao.
The mentionable name is not the eternal name.

Tangle of confusion

Clinging to intellectual definitions and concepts is the reason why the free spirit is channelled into pre-defined paths. The mind loses its natural clarity and incarcerates itself in the confusion of its discriminating, conceptual thinking. Overcoming this sorrowful state is the basic element of Zen.

One day, a monk came to Zen Master Tokusan (twelfth century) to ask him about the truth of Zen. In accordance with Buddhist regulations he bowed deeply before his master prior to asking his question. But before he had finished bowing, Tokusan gave him a violent blow with the stick.

"Why are you hitting me?" asked the monk, with a pain-distorted face, "I haven't said anything yet."

"There would be no point in waiting for you to open your mouth", said Tokusan and raised his stick, ready for the next blow. The monk quickly took leave.

Zen is always refreshingly direct and does not digress in pleasant words and friendly fussings, aimed at uplifting the ego. It is all just about letting go of all concepts and thoughts. The truth beyond all words will only reveal itself to us when we become completely free from all intellectual concepts. Zen Master Fo-yan (twelfth century) thus gives us the following good advice:

Whoever does not stop and turn his gaze inwards will continue to search for rational explanations. This searching and comparing done by the intellect is utterly wrong. If people would turn their awareness in on itself, they would understand everything.

In this great liberation we will become aware of our true essence, based on an understanding which surpasses all the power and ability of our thinking.

Chapter 16

Zen - The Path of Personal Experience

Perceiving the moment

A true Zen master will constantly strive to liberate the student from his intellectual refuse. Over and over again he will try to lead him directly to the truth of Zen. With all available means, often of a physical nature, the Chinese Zen masters of old shattered the whole tangled web of intellectual concepts and explanations. Their aim was to lead the student to the reality of his true being with uncompromising directness. One day, the Chinese Zen Master Shih-kung (ninth century) asked his highest monk the following question:

"Can you grasp empty space?" The monk replied, "Yes master." "How then?" asked the master. The monk immediately stretched out his arm and grasped at the emptiness. Hereupon the master remarked, "How can you grasp empty space in this way?" – "How else?"

countered the monk. Hardly had he finished asking when, with lightning speed, the master grabbed the monk's nose and gave it a hard twist. The monk shrieked in pain and cried out, "Oh, Ah, you're really hurting me!" The master let go of his nose and said, "There is no way you can grasp empty space."

If an individual, like the monk in our example, claims to have attained something, it is a sure sign of error, for in Zen, there is nothing to attain and nothing to achieve. There is only a "mysterious, silent understanding" and nothing more.

The truth of Zen is simple and direct. It is found precisely in the most ordinary things of everyday life. Reality is always present – at this very moment! The mystery and wonder of Zen lies in drinking a glass of water or tying shoelaces. An old Zen saying goes:

Miraculous deeds and acts full of wonder! I draw water and carry firewood.

However, this is only evident to those of us who experience things in the present moment. That is why Zen tells us, "Seize the moment and be Now-Here!" In other words: "See everything as the one truth, and do not cling to the patterns of your dualistic and limited points of view!"

Powerful teaching method

Zen is a life without chains, a life in freedom and freedom itself. Break your self-made chains of the small clinging ego, and the true Self will radiate forth in all its glory – all-encompassing and all-pervading! This, our original, true being is completely free, without the slightest distinction or polarity. It is omnipresent, silent and pure, and manifests itself as mysterious, peaceful joy. It is the whole perfection of divine being, which is with us every moment of our lives without our being aware of it.

In the encounter between master and student, the master constantly endeavours to help the student directly experience his true being. In their powerful way, the old Chinese masters often treated their students in an extremely harsh way, yet always tempered with loving kindness.

A monk asked Zen Master Ma-tsu, "What is the truth of Zen?" With a tremendous blow to the chest, Ma-tsu instantly knocked him to the ground and roared, "If I hadn't struck you down, the whole country would laugh at me."

Ma-tsu was one of the most significant and most capable Zen masters of the Tang dynasty. His powerful and direct teaching methods led many of his students to enlightenment. Ma-tsu's most notable disciple was Pai-chang, who later became the master of the Zen giant, Huang-po. Ma-tsu's hands-on teaching method became the trigger for Pai-chang's "Great Awakening".

> One day, Pai-chang was with his master Ma-tsu in the garden behind the house. As they saw a flock of wild geese cross the sky, Ma-tsu asked, "What was that?"
> "Wild geese, master."
> "Where have they flown to?" asked Ma-tsu.
> "They have simply flown away, master."
> Ma-tsu suddenly grabbed Pai-chang's nose and twisted it hard. Overcome with pain, Pai-chang cried out loudly, "Ow, ow!"
> "You say they have flown away," said Ma-tsu, "yet how can it be that they have been here from the very beginning?"
> Sweat broke out from Pai-chang's every pore; he was enlightened on the spot.

Ma-tsu's behaviour must seem strange and puzzling to those who have no insight into the truth of Zen. Rational thinkers, who primarily use their intellects to judge Zen, consider it to be utterly illogical and absurd.

The basis for understanding Zen is and will always be our individual experience and not long-winded explanations. Mere belief in the truth inherent in us and an intellectual understanding will not help us at all. We must actually live and see it for ourselves.

The truth we are seeking has always been here; it is just that we are not here. That is the only problem. Yet right now, in this moment, our true being reveals itself here. If we do not find it here we will find it nowhere.

Zen Master Joshu was once asked:

"What is right before your own eyes?"

Joshu answered, "You."

Chapter 17

The Sword of Non-Discriminating Wisdom

The directness of Zen

Zen is the height and the quintessence of the whole of Buddhism. It is the direct, immediate way to liberation from imprisonment within the circle of birth and death.

Zen takes the sword of "non-discriminating wisdom" and at one fell swoop slices through the Gordian knot of our spiritual confusion. In the powerful words of Zen Master Hsueh-tou from the eleventh century:

> Where the sword of wisdom flies, sun and moon lose their shine and heaven and earth lose their colour.
> Through this experience the devils' bellies burst and the eye of transcendental wisdom opens to you.

Right now, in this instant, take the sword of wisdom and shatter the bonds of your intellectual interpretations. Shatter all attachments to the interwoven memories of your dead past. Cast off instantly all discriminating conceptual thinking and you are free. The whole delusion of your fixed concepts of body, mind and world, of space and time and of birth and death falls apart, and the boundless expanse of the One Mind shines forth. This is exactly what distinguishes Zen from all other religious systems and philosophical teachings.

To remove a tree, Zen does not start by clipping the smallest of the leaves. One little leaf and then another. And then there is another and yet another, and then the little twigs and so on, until reaching the bottom. Even before arriving at the bottom, everything has already grown back again at the top and we start all over again. This is not the way of Zen. With the sharply-honed sword of non-discriminating wisdom Zen fells the whole tree in a single stroke. This is the true method of Zen; this is "the direct path to liberation". In the words of Zen Master Huang-po:

The mind is filled with radiant clarity, so cast off the darkness of your old, dead concepts. Free yourself of everything!

The only way we can rid ourselves of this whole problem is when we discard ourselves, which means that the causing factor must be eliminated. And the causing factor is nothing other than the ego. The ego is the end-product of the three "kleshas," the three basic errors: greed, hatred and blindness, in other words, desire, rejection and ignorance. The three kleshas interact to create the delusion of an independently existing personality. Yet this amounts to no more than a deception – a delusion, lacking any reality whatsoever.

Follow me "now"

How long do we want to continue playing this game? Why not let everything go, and awaken? – Now! The best opportunity is right now. There is no other and no better opportunity than "Now". We should not end up like the young man who comes and asks Jesus what he must do to become his disciple and Jesus says to him:

> "Come and follow me!" And the young man replies, "Alright, but I'm afraid it won't be right away because I have a lot to do, for my father has died and I must bury him first. I must order

the grave, organise the funeral service, then I have to ..." And Jesus interrupts him and says, "Verily I say to you, let the dead bury their own and come follow me!"

In other words: Follow me "now"! Now! Not some other time, not tomorrow or the day after, for only Now exists. The direct Zen way is not a way for the small-minded. So why wait? Why say: "Today I've made another step in the right direction, some things

seem a little clearer, and someday ...?" No! Forget someday! There is no someday. Past and future are no more than thoughts that appear in the mind in the present moment. Thus the experience of time is nothing else than thinking, and therefore, time is illusory and non-existent. There is only "Now" and nothing else.

Right now, in this instant, our original true being reveals itself – nothing could be closer. So therefore, immerse yourself in it "Now-Here"! There is no other way.

Chapter 18

Instant Perception of the Truth

The goose in the bottle

Individual experience is everything in Zen and so it is absolutely necessary that we stop dreaming. This means that we stop projecting, so that we no longer see things through the stencils of our limited world-view.

All our well-worn dualistic thinking habits, together with our subjective beliefs have created an environment in which we have trapped ourselves and can no longer escape. We have trapped ourselves in our self-made entanglement of discriminating, conceptual thinking. We have turned ourselves into the goose in the bottle and have been taken in by the philosopher Ryoku as in the following Zen encounter:

One day, the highly learned philosopher Ryoku goes to the Chinese Zen Master Nansen, who lived in the ninth century and says: "There is a problem which has been bothering me for a long time. Can you please help me to solve it?"

"Alright then, go ahead," says Master Nansen.

Ryoku begins: "Well, imagine that you have a large bottle with an opening just big enough for you to be able to lower a goose egg into it. After a time, the egg hatches and a goose chick comes out. The chick grows bigger and bigger until one day there is a fully-grown goose in the

bottle. Now I would like to ask you: how would you free the goose from the bottle without breaking the bottle or harming the goose?"

Master Nansen remains silent for a moment ... Then suddenly he bellows, "Ryoku!!!" so loudly that the philosopher jumps back, deep in shock. "Yes, Master?"

And Master Nansen says, "Look, the goose is free!"

The philosopher had trapped himself so hopelessly in his self-fabricated entanglement of discriminating thought that he had turned himself into the goose in the bottle. That is why, in Zen practice, we must recognise that the bottle – meaning our self-made dualistic limitations – is merely a projection of discriminating thought. In the end, it is a matter of seeing clearly, awakening step by step and becoming more aware, and then finally, completely awakening. As long as we dream, we are caught in our dream – like the goose in the bottle. But when we awaken, there is neither goose nor bottle.

Projections

So let us not deceive ourselves by trusting in our intellectual knowledge and by seeking here and there for the truth. All we need do is to refrain from discriminating, conceptual thinking. Therefore, leave everything as it is, and everything is fine! For what we have constantly before us each moment is the boundless One Mind in all its perfection. Free yourself of everything, whatever it may be and the reality of your true being will reveal itself. This is the way of instantly perceiving the truth.

However, our spiritual ignorance produces an endless multitude of thought waves on the self-existing reality of the One Mind. These waves manifest themselves into the multitudinous forms of an apparent external phenomenal world that we then take for reality and in which we entangle ourselves. Thus we fail to realise that the world as we perceive it, is just our own projection. It is nothing more than a projection of the discriminating consciousness of accepting and rejecting.

Absolutely everything we encounter is in truth the One Mind, beside which nothing else exists. Everything is the all-embracing wholeness of divine being in its absolute completeness. And everything imperfect, or rather what we perceive as imperfect, is nothing other than our own projection. We project our conditioned, dualistic values we believe in, cover the perceived object with them, and then believe that what we see is the thing itself. But that is indeed not the case.

It is just the same as if we would see a snake at night in the moonlight lying alongside a path. Horrified, we jump back and run away. Yet the next day when it is light and we pass along the same way, we see that it was only a rope. The sunlight of clear realisation shows us the truth, so that we see things as they are. Nothing is projected onto it and we perceive everything as it is. Everything we perceive as long as we live in the dream of Samsara, the dream of an apparent external world of phenomena, is our own projection. It is thus mere appearance, devoid of true being. For true being obtains its being of itself – there is no beginning and there is no end. There is neither birth nor ageing, illness, pain, nor death. There is only inexpressible reality, beside which nothing else exists.

Chapter 19

The Radiating Reality of the Mind

Beyond speaking and silence

All discrimination in terms of good and bad, sacred and profane is a result of our ignorance. When Bodhidharma, the legendary first patriarch of Zen was asked by the Chinese Emperor Wu from Liang, "What is the most sacred in the world?" he replied, "Vast emptiness, nothing sacred." We must leave everything behind us: Buddha, enlightenment, dharma, Zen, whatever it may be. All these concepts are merely empty word-shells and of no use whatsoever.

As long as we still cling to words, we can never arrive at directly experiencing our true being. Therefore, Zen requires us to negate absolutely everything then transcend even this negation too. As long as we still have the smallest trace of negation or affirmation in us, we are still a thousand miles apart from the truth of Zen. Whoever opens his mouth to affirm or negate is lost. He is completely outside of Zen. In the words of Zen Master Bassui from the fourteenth century:

Whatever you say is wrong. And if you say

nothing, it is equally wrong.

And in one of his dharma talks, the Chinese Zen Master I-tuan (tenth century) said:

> "Speech is blasphemy, silence misleading. Above speech and silence there is a way which leads to boundlessness, but my mouth is not wide enough to point you to it." With these words he arose from his high chair and departed.

In Zen there is nothing but radical self-detachment and self-dissolution into the original condition of the mind – here and now. Yet when we have achieved complete realisation, we will experience nothing other than this omnipresent buddha-essence which has been constantly with us as the silent observer behind all experience. That which constitutes the fundament of our experience – the pure consciousness behind all experiences – was constantly with us, but we were not there. In the words of Meister Eckhart:

> God is within, but you are without.

In this crystal-clear awareness we will realise that all

we achieved on our spiritual path was no more than a mass of empty husks. We have only been playing with empty husks and we have not experienced the essence itself.

We cannot find our true Self through books and scholarliness because it lies beyond all words, beyond thought. We can study and memorise all the revelations of the old masters and know all the corresponding commentaries. The moment we suddenly awaken to the radiating truth of the Mind we will experience that all of this was nothing more than chaff, of no true value.

The thunder of silence

We can only experience our true being beyond birth and death when the mind is empty and clear, without thoughts and concepts. When we have silenced our autonomous compulsive thinking, we will no longer produce the slightest trace of attachment and karma. Then we will already achieve complete freedom in this life.

Yet ruled by our autonomous compulsive thinking, we live in a state of separateness within a world of self-created problems and conflicts. It is just like the dog in the hall of mirrors. It only sees its own projections, to which it reacts with aggression and fear.

We are so identified with our intellect that we do not even realise that it makes us its slave. Since we are identified with the intellect, we derive our sense of self from it and fear that we will cease to exist if we stop thinking. Breaking this self-generated vicious circle by realising spiritual clarity is the real aim of Zen.

Zen opens our eyes to the great mystery of our universal Essence. It opens a path to the unending inner space which manifests itself to us in its boundless expanse beyond space and perpetuity beyond time. If the term "radically empirical" applies to anything at all, then it applies with certainty to Zen. Zen is a matter of absolute experience in every respect. Take, for example, the following occurrence from the ninth century:

One day as the Chinese Zen Master Ting-chou was crossing a bridge, he encountered three highly learned Buddhist scholars. One of the scholars wished to test Zen Master Ting's understanding of Zen and asked him: "The river is deep and its depths must be plumbed. What does this mean?"

The questioner had hardly finished speaking when Master Ting grabbed him with both hands and was about to throw him from the bridge. The other two scholars held him back and cried, "Stop! Have you gone mad? Let him go right away!"

Ting released the scholar and said, "If you had not held me back I would have let him plumb the depths of the river himself!"

The highest truth is beyond all words and concepts, beyond all notions, all acceptance and rejection. It is beyond everything. So free yourself from the autonomous compulsion of discriminating, conceptual thinking. Free yourself of all concepts and the boundless expanse of the One Mind will manifest itself to you as the "thunder of silence" that shakes the entire universe.

The veil of our spiritual blindness, which has obscured the perception of our original, true being, tears apart from top to bottom. In a stroke, the eye of enlightenment has opened and for the first time, we see reality just as it is.

A list of Zen masters

The names of the masters given in this list conform to the spelling used in the book. Following this is the Pinyin transcription, where relevant, as well as the Japanese spelling.

Ba-ling (10th century); Baling Haojian, Jap. Haryo Kokan

Basho (1644-1694); Jap. Matsuo Basho

Bassui (1327-1387); Jap. Bassui Tokusho Zenji

Bodhidharma (470-543); Jap. Daruma

Buddha (563-483 B.C..); Skrt. Buddha Shakyamuni, Jap. Butsu

Bukko (1226-1286); Wuxue Zuyuan, Jap. Bukko Kokushi

Chang-ching (854-932); Changquing Huileng, Jap. Chokei Eryo

Chang-sha (died 868); Changsha Jingcen, Jap. Cho-sha Keijin

Chia-men (died 1031); Kuang-tsu, Jap. Chimon Koso

Chia-shan (805-881); Jiashan Shanhui, Jap. Kassan

Chih-yüan (died about 1150); Zhiyuan Kuoan

Chü-chih (9th century); Jinhua Juzhi, Jap. Chikan Gutei

Chung-i (8th/9th century); Zhongyi Hongen, Jap. Chuyu

Da-long (870-940); Dalong Zhihong, Jap. Dairyo Chiko

Dan-yüan (8th/9th century); Danyuan Yingzhen, Jap. Tangen Oshin

Dogen Zenji (13th century); Jap. Dogen Kigen

Dong-shan (807-869); Dongshan Liangjie, Jap. Tozan Ryokai

Fa-yen (885-958); Fayan Wenyi, Jap. Hogen Buneki

Fen-yang (947-1024); Fenyang Shanzhao, Jap. Funyo Zensho

Fo-yan (1067-1120); Foyan Qingyuan, Jap. Butsugen

Fu Ta-shih (497-569); Fu Dashi, Jap. Fu Daishi

Ganto (828-887); Yantou Quanhuo, Jap. Ganto Zenkatsu

Guizong (died 979); Guizong Cezhen, Jap. Kiso Sakushin

Hakuin (1686-1769); Jap. Hakuin Ekaku Zenji

Hong-zhi (1091-1157); Hongzhi Zhengjue, Jap. Wanshi Shogaku

Hotei (10th century); Budai, Jap. Hotei

Hsiang-yen (died 898); Xiangyan Zhixian, Jap. Kyogen Chikan

Hsing-hua (830-888); Xinghua Congjiang, Jap. Koke Zonsho

Hsing-shan (815-885); Xingshan Jianhong

Hsüan-sha (835-908); Xuansha Shibe, Jap. Gensha Shibi

Hsü-yün (1840-1959); Xuyun

Hsüeh-tou (980-1052); Xuedou Chongxian, Jap. Setcho Juken

Huang-long (1002-1069); Huanglong Huinan, Jap. Oryo (Oryu) Enan

Huang-po (died 850); Huangbo Xiyuan, Jap. Obaku

Hui-chung (ca. 675-775); Nanyang Huizhong, Jap. Nanyo Echu

Hui-neng (638-713); Dajian Huineng, Jap. Daikan Eno

Joshu (778-897); Zhaozhou Congshen, Jap. Joshu Jushin

Lao-tse (6th century B.C.)

Lin-chi (died 866); Linji Yixuan, Jap. Rinzai Gigen

Ling-yün (9th century); Lingyun Zhiqin, Jap. Reiun Shigon

Ma-tsu (709-788); Mazu Daoyi, Jap. Baso Doitsu

Mu-chou (ca. 780-877); Muzhou Daozong, Jap. Bokushu Doshu

Mumon (1183-1260); Wumen Huikai, Jap. Mumon Ekai

Nansen (748-835); Nanquan Puyuan, Jap. Nansen Fugan

Nan-yüeh (677-744); Nanyue Huairang, Jap. Nangaku Ejo

Pai-chang (720-814); Baizhang Huaihai, Jap. Hyakujo Ekai

Pan-shan (8th/9th century); Panshan Baoji, Jap. Banzan Hoshaku

Pang-yün (740-808); Pangyun, Jap. Ho Un

Pao-che (8th/9th century); Magu Baozhe, Jap. Mayoku Hotetsu

Pao-chi (9th century); Baoji Xiujing, Jap. Hoji Kyujo

Po-chan (1575-1630); Bozhan

Pu-hua (died 860); Puhua Pu-ko, Jap. Fuke

Ryokan Daigu (1758-1831); Jap. Ryokan Daigu

Ryutan (8th/9th century); Longtan Chongxin, Jap. Ryutan Soshin

San-sheng (9th century); Sansheng Huiran, Jap. Sansho Enen

Seppo (822-908); Xuefeng Yicun, Jap. Seppo Gison

Shih-Kung (9th century)

Shih-tou (700-790); Shitou Xiqian, Jap. Sekito Kisen

Tao-hsin (580-651); Daoxin, Jap. Doshin

Ta-hui (1089-1163); Dahui Zonggao, Jap. Daie Soko

Ta-yü (9th century); Gaoan Dayu, Jap. Koan Daigu

Tien-lung (8th/9th century); Tianlong

Ting-chou (9th century); Ding Shangzuo, Jap. Jo Joza

Tokusan (782-865); Deshan Xuanjian, Jap. Tokusan Senkan

Tou-dsi (819-914); Touzi Datong, jap. Tosu Daido

Tou-shuai (1044-1091); Doushuai Congyue, jap.

Tosotsu Juetsu

Tsao-shan (840-901); Caoshan Benji, jap. Sozan Honjaku

Tung-shan (910-990); Dongshan Shouchu, jap. Tozan Shusho

Wei-shan (771-853); Weishan Lingyu, jap. Isan Reiyu

Yang-chi (992-1049); Yangqi Fanghui, jap. Yogi Hoe

Yang-shan (807-883); Yangshan Huiji, jap. Kyozan Ejaku

Yen-kuan (750-842); Yanguan Qian, jap. Enkan Seian

Yeshugin Kenshin (6th century)

Ying-an (1103-1163); Yingan Tanhua, jap. Oan Donge

Yong-ming (904-975); Yongming Yanshou, jap. Yomei

Yüan-wu (1063-1135); Yuanwu Keqin, jap. Engo Kokugon

Yüeh-shan (745-828); Yueshan Weiyan, jap. Yakusan

Yün-chu (died ca. 902); Yunzhu Daoying, jap. Ungo Doyo

Yün-men (864-949); Yunmen Wenyan, jap. Ummon

Yün-yen (ca. 781-841); Yunyan Tansheng, jap. Ungan Donjo

Yung-chia (665-713); Yongjia Xuanjue, jap. Yoka Genkaku

Zuigan Shigen (9th century); Ruiyan Shiyan, jap. Zuigan

Glossary

Adi-Buddha, Samantabhadra, Sanskrit, Original-buddha, absolute reality as the highest being in Tibetan-Buddhist cosmology. He is regarded as the personification of pure →Shunyata.

His →mantra is: OM AH HUM, which represents the body, speech and mind of all buddhas. Samantabhadra (Chin. Pu-hsien, Jap. Fugen), literally, "He of all-embracing kindness" is of great significance in Mahayana-Buddhism. He is seen as the embodiment of the equality of unity and diversity. He is the protector of all those who preach the dharma.

Advaita-Vedanta Sanskrit, is one of the three major philosophical, theological systems in Hindu Vedanta. Its main leading exponent was Shankara (ninth century), one of India's greatest sages and philosophers. The Advaita-Vedanta teaches that the divine Universal Mind →Brahman, the Self →Atman and the external world of phenomena are utterly one. In Shankara's Viveka-Chudamani, "The Crest-jewel of Discrimination" it is written, "You are Brahman, pure consciousness, the observer of all experiences, and your true being is bliss."

Amida Jap. for →Amitabha (Sanskrit)

Amitabha Sanskrit, "Boundless light," Jap. "Amida". One of the most important buddhas in →Mahayana Buddhism. It is the buddha of "western paradise" →Sukhavati, not linked to a particular location but instead meaning a state of consciousness of boundless light, love and comprehension. According to the teachings of Shin-Buddhism, anyone who in deep faith calls Amitabha's name (especially at the hour of death), will be reborn in Sukhavati paradise. In the "Pure Land school," this call is known as Namu Amida Butsu, "worship of the buddha Amitabha" →Nembutsu.

Anitya Sanskrit, literally: "impermanence, transitoriness". In Buddhism, one of the three characteristics of all conditional arising and thus all being. Everything that has arisen, dwells for a while and then decays once again – it arises, exists and decays. Impermanence is the fundamental law of the whole of existence. The two other characteristics are derived from this: "Non-substantiality (Anatman)" and "Suffering (Duhkha)".

Atman Sanskrit. In Hinduism it is the immortal true Self of mankind. As absolute consciousness it is the impartial observer behind all experiences and identical with →Brahman.

Avalokiteshvara Sanskrit, "the lord who looks down upon all things, or who hears the cries of the world". He is the →Bodhisattva of compassion and embodies all-encompassing compassion (→Karuna) with all suffering beings. His byname is "Mahakaruna," great mercy, one of the main facets of a buddha. The other main facet of a buddha is wisdom (→Prajna), which is embodied in a special way by Bodhisattva →Manjushri. Avalokiteshvara's boundless compassion is seen in his constant readiness to help all those beings who turn to him in their suffering. In Tibet, Avalokiteshvara is revered as →Chenresi, in China as →Kuan-yin and in Japan as →Kannon (also Kwannon or Kanzeon).

Avatamsaka-Sutra Sanskrit →Hua-yen

Avidya Sanskrit, literally: "ignorance, non-recognising". Avidya is considered to be the root cause for the attachment to →samsara – the cycle of birth and death. Ignorance is the root of all suffering, for it is that state of mind which is not in accordance with reality. In →Mahayana Buddhism, Avidya is denoted as non-recognition of the voidness (→Shunyata) of all things. Thus, non-recognition of the deceptive nature of all phenomena is the true reason for all suffering.

Bardo Tibetan, literally: "intermediate state," relates to the intermediate state between death and reincarnation. Buddhist teaching strongly stresses the direction-defining force of the state of mind of a dying person (virtuous, not-virtuous or neutral) and also the negative influences of greed, hatred and ignorance during bardo itself.

Beginner's mind →Shoshin

Bodhi Sanskrit, literally: "Awakening, enlightenment". →Satori

Bodhichitta Sanskrit, "Enlightenment-Mind", the endeavour to achieve enlightenment for the good of all beings in order to free them from suffering. Also, the direct term for the enlightened mind itself.

Bodhidharma, Sanskrit, (Jap. Daruma, Chin. Tao-mo). The 28th patriarch after →Buddha Shakyamuni in India and the first Chinese patriarch of Zen. Since he came from India, lying to the West from a Chinese viewpoint, he was also known as "the barbarian from the West". Bodhidharma is a Zen figure shrouded in mystery and very little is known about him. He is the symbol of several characteristics of Zen and the object of the constantly recurring question in the →mondos: "What is the reason why Bodhidharma came from the West?" The question means as much as: What is the highest truth? What is my true being? Who am I? What is the essence of the innermost being of Zen? The question "Why did Bodhidharma come from the West?" has received over two hundred answers in Zen. Here are some examples:

A monk asked Hsiang-lin: "With which intention did Bodhidharma come from the West?" Hsiang-lin replied, "Too much sitting makes one very exhausted." To the same question Chiu Feng replied, "An inch of tortoise hair weighs nine pounds."

And Tung Shan's answer to Lung Ya was, "I shall tell you as soon as the mountain stream flows upwards."

Bodhisattva Sanskrit, literally: "Enlightenment-being". A person who, having reached enlightenment (→Satori), spends his life in the service of others to help them reach liberation. The term Bodhisattva is often used to denote a future →buddha.

Brahman Sanskrit, the one, eternal, all-pervading absolute, origin and bearer of the entire universe. The philosophy of Vedanta (→Advaita-Vedanta) teaches that Brahman – the Absolute, surpassing the personal level and →Atman, the true Self in all beings are one. Brahman, the sole existing truth, is the essence and the Self (Atman) of all being.

The Viveka-Chudamani, one of the most significant texts of Advaita-Vedanta says: "Atman is one with Brahman. This is the highest truth: Only Brahman is real. There is nothing else besides it. When it has been recognised as highest reality, there exists nothing else besides Brahman." This insight that Brahman and Atman are one is regarded as the highest goal, since it brings liberation from the imprisonment in →samsara, the cycle of birth and death.

Buddha Sanskrit, literally: "the awakened one". 1. The historical Buddha Shakyamuni, who was born in India in ca. 563 B.C. 2. A person who has fulfilled complete enlightenment (→satori), liberating him from the cycle of birth and death (→samsara). 3. The final truth, the true nature of all being.

Buddha-Dharma Sanskrit (Jap. Buppo), "buddha-law". The teachings of the historical Buddha

183

Shakyamuni. In Zen however, we do not denote buddha-dharma as the teaching that can be conveyed in words, rather it is the highest truth, which is inaccessible for discriminating, conceptual thinking. It is that essential truth which led to Buddha's teachings and which can only be conceived in direct comprehension, in the experience of enlightenment (→satori).

Buddha-Nature Skt., "Buddhata," the true nature of all beings, which makes it possible for a person to reach enlightenment (→satori).

Chakra Sanskrit →Kundalini

Chan Chin. for Zen (Jap.)

Chenresi Tibetan, literally: "the lord who does not turn away from suffering". The Tibetan form of →Boddhisattva's →Avalokiteshvara. The most often recited →mantra in Tibet, →OM MANI PADME HUM is dedicated to it.

Cycle of birth and death →samsara

Daigo-Tettei Jap. literally: "Great →Satori, which

reaches down to the ground". Highest complete enlightenment. One of its principle characteristics is the experience of empty vastness and the lifting of all contrariety with the destruction of the small "I". Furthermore, the experience that the whole universe and the Self-Mind are completely identical.

Dharma Sanskrit, a term with various meanings. The teachings of →Buddha. Universal order and its laws. In this book, mainly used in the sense of the teachings of →Zen.

Dharmakaya Sanskrit, "Body of the great Order". The indescribable true being of the →buddhas, and at the same time, the essence of the universe.

Dorje Tibetan, "Diamond". →Vajra

Dzogchen Tibetan →Mahamudra

Enlightenment →Satori, →Bodhi

Enlightenment-Mind →Bodhichitta

Great Death →Satori

Hara Jap., literally: "Belly, abdomen". This common Zen term signifies the area approximately three finger widths below the belly button as the centre of all being. It is the centre of every person and at the same time the centre of the universe. Through the practice of →zazen and correct breathing a great energy and power develop in this centre. Hara, as the centre of energy, is in Zen the point of origin of all activity (as in the meaning of "acting on intuition," but in Zen its meaning goes much deeper).

Hinayana Sanskrit, "small vehicle". Oldest school of the two main branches of Buddhism. The original derogatory term "small vehicle" originates from the exponents of the later school of →Mahayana Buddhism. The main endeavour of Hinayana Buddhists is to reach their own liberation from →samsara, the cycle of birth and death. Here, little consideration is made for liberating other beings from the sea of suffering of samsara. In the rescue boot of the small vehicle there is only room for one person. Hinayana is viewed as the first step of Buddha's teachings. Only later did →Buddha reveal the complete teachings of Mahayana.

Hishiryo Jap., literally: "that which thinking cannot

fathom". Zen term for →Enlightenment, which eludes all understanding through conceptual thought and thus transcends thinking.

Ho! Chin. This powerful, loud cry is often used by Zen masters as an abrupt means of expression to shatter the fixated, discriminating thinking of the student.

Hua-yen Chin., (Jap. Kegon, Skt. Avatamsaka), literally: "floral decorations" or "garland"; originally the name of a comprehensive →Mahayana text. The Hua-yen is seen by many Chinese and Japanese Buddhists as the crown of all Buddhist teachings and the perfection of Buddhist thought and realisation. Hua-yen is the doctrine of holistic being, and at the same time, a synthesis of all major Mahayana thinking. In Hua-yen, the universal One Mind is compared with the endless surface of the ocean, in which all things and events in mutual pervasion are an all-encompassing whole, which contains everything within itself. Everything is in perfect harmony together, for everything is the manifestation of the one principle – similar to the waves on the ocean. Everything in the universe, whether animate or not, is thus the One Mind, beside which nothing else exists.

Ishin-Denshin Jap., literally: "to transmit Mind by means of Mind". A fundamental concept of →Zen, often translated as "transmission of Heart-Mind to Heart-Mind". The term originates from the Platform Sutra by the sixth patriarch Hui-neng. In this →sutra, Hui-neng explains that the truth of Zen can only be realised through one's own experience, in a direct understanding of its true nature. Scholarliness gained through reading is worthless – thus Hui-neng's act of tearing apart the sutras. Zen Master Huang-po says "There is no understanding through words, but merely a transmission from Mind to Mind."

Joriki Jap. The power of concentration gained through Zen meditation (→zazen).

Kannon, Kanzeon or also Kwannon, Jap. for →Bodhisattva →Avalokiteshvara.

Karma Sanskrit, literally: "Action or deed". The law of cause and effect, by which all thoughts and actions have a corresponding consequence. Through this we determine the quality of our own lives and influence that of others.

Karuna Sanskrit, literally: "compassion", all-embracing compassion. One of the two principal virtues in →Mahayana Buddhism; the other being →Prajna. (→Avalokiteshvara)

Kensho Jap., seeing one's own nature. →Satori

Kinhin Jap., The practice of walking meditation, which is usually performed for ten to fifteen minutes between the individual →zazen periods of sitting. In traditional →Rinzai Zen the walking pace is quick and brisk, in →Soto Zen, on the other hand it is very slow. Some contemporary Zen masters often set a tempo which lies between these two forms.

Koan Jap., literally: "public notice" (Chin. Kung-an). In Zen, the term for a paradox quote from a Zen master that points to the ultimate truth. A koan is there to aid a student of Zen in overcoming discriminating dualistic thinking so that he reaches the truth beyond all thinking. Koans play an important role in Zen instruction. A koan contains a question for which there is no answer for the intellect. To solve it, a higher intuition (→Prajna) is required. However, a koan is everything but a puzzle, since it requires the student to abandon his faith in his own, habitual way of understanding. The answer lies beyond logic and it is there to aid the student to break through to the enlightened clarity of the Mind (→Satori).

The striking aspect of all koans is the alogicalness, the paradoxicalness of the words or the action. When one reads the answers of the old Zen masters to their students' questions, emanating from the Zen mind, one is confused and asks oneself what in fact the answer has to do with the question. It must be said here that these statements of the Zen masters have nothing to do with conceptual or intellectual ascertainments within our habitual limits of logical dualism. Instead we are dealing here with the manifestation of a tremendous experience of such all-encompassing universality that within it, all limitations of space and time and all language barriers are transcended.

Kuan-yin, Chin. for →Avalokiteshvara

Kundalini Sanskrit, "Snake power". The spiritual energy in every person which rests in the Muladhara chakra at the lower end of the spine. When awakened, it rises up through the spine and pervades the individual chakras (centres of subtle, delicate energy), until it reaches the thousand-petalled lotus of the Sahasrara chakra directly above the top of the head. Ultimately, at this point, in the seventh centre, beyond the coarser material body, this cosmic energy unites with the Divine.

Lila Sanskrit, literally: "Game". In Hinduism, Lila is the divine game in the world of phenomena. The whole of creation is described as God's game.

Mahamudra Sanskrit, "Great symbol". The principle teaching of the Kagyu school of Tibetan →Vajrayana Buddhism. Mahamudra is also translated as the "great seal". This expresses the significance of finality, as with a seal. Similar to the practise of →Dzogchen in the Nyingma line, Mahamudra practise is about directly perceiving the light-nature of the Mind and thus reaching enlightenment (→Satori).

Mahayana Sanskrit, literally: "Great vehicle," as opposed to the earlier orthodox school of →"Hinayana". Mahayana Buddhism attaches a much greater importance to all-embracing compassion (Karuna) and the wish to help all beings reach liberation than it does to abstinence. Mahayana also includes the helping power of the →buddhas and →bodhisattvas.

Mahayana-Buddhism, Mahayana teachings →Mahayana

Maitreya Sanskrit (Jap. Miroku), literally: "The all-loving one". One of the five earthly →buddhas, the embodiment of all-embracing love. The Mahayana Buddhists anticipate that this, the last earthly buddha, currently abiding in Tusita Heaven, will come as a teacher of the worlds in around thirty thousand years' time.

Maitri Sanskrit, literally: "Goodness and mercy". One of the prime virtues in Buddhism. It is charitable goodness towards all beings, free from all attachments.

Maitri-Karuna literally: "Goodness and compassion". Fundamental state of mind of a →Bodhisattva, which is expressed in his desire to lead all beings to liberation.

Makyo Jap., approx. "devilish phenomena," deceptive, distracting phenomena and sensations which can arise during Zen meditation (→zazen). Makyos can appear in a variety of forms; as wonderful sounds, smells, faces, prophetic visions, sometimes also as levitation. However, Makyos are quite harmless as long as the zazen practitioner takes no heed of them and continues his practise unperturbed.

Manjushri Sanskrit (Jap. Monju), literally: "He who is noble and kindly". One of the most important →Bodhisattvas in →Mahayana Buddhism. Manjushri is the embodiment of wisdom. He is most commonly depicted with his sword of wisdom, cutting through ignorance. His raging Tantric appearance is that of the bull-headed Yamantaka, the vanquisher of death.

Mantra Sanskrit, one or a series of syllables, filled with spiritual energy, which the student recites either verbally or in the mind. Constantly repeating a mantra leads to realisation of the true being by way of purification of the thoughts. However, a mantra is only endowed with transforming powers when one has received it directly from the master (→OM MANI PADME HUM).

Mara Sanskrit, Pali, literally: "Murderer, destroyer (of life)". Mara is the personification of the obstacles on the road to liberation. As the tempter and the phenomenon of unwholesomeness, he can be compared with the Christian devil, the "Father of lies". His three daughters act as his helpers: Rati – desire, Avati – discontentment, and Tanha – greed. In addition, Mara is supported by a whole army of demons.

Maya Sanskrit, literally: "Illusion, semblance, deception". In Vedanta philosophy (→Vedanta) Maya is the power of great illusion. It veils one's view so that one is unable to recognise →Brahman, ultimate reality. Shankara links Maya to →Avidya, ignorance. Ignorance, that is, non-perception of the ultimate reality of Brahman, creates the delusion of an external world of phenomena in space and time by means of its obscurement. →Mahayana Buddhism characterises Maya as a deception or illusion, just like a phantasm created by a mirage. Individual things are fleeting and have no existence of their own, they are in fact void (→Shunyata) and mere concepts.

Ming-Dynasty Chinese epoch from 1368 – 1644

Mondo Jap., "question-answer" (Chin. "Wen-ta"), a dialogue between Zen master and student, also often just between masters. In answer to a question concerning Buddhist truth or an existential problem, the student normally receives a paradox (→Koan), which cannot be classified by the intellect. The aim behind this is to smash the bounds of discriminating, conceptual thinking so that the student can obtain an answer from his innermost intuition (Heart-Mind). A very well-known Mondo is: A Zen monk asked

Zen Master Joshu: "What is the meaning of the first patriarch's coming from the West?" Joshu said: "The cypress tree in the courtyard."

Mu Jap. (Chin. Wu), literally: "Nothing, non-being, is not, has not, un-, none". One of the central concepts of →Zen and →Taoism. It describes utter freedom from all identification and attachment, and also stands for realisation of the void (→Shunyata). In the well-known Koan collection of the Mumonkan we encounter "Mu" in the first example, "Joshu's dog". In Zen it is also known as "the →koan Mu". "A monk respectfully asked Master Joshu: 'Does a dog have Buddha-Nature or not?' Joshu answered: 'Mu'".

Master Joshu's reply is simply "nothingness," which does not imply that a dog does not have →buddha-nature. Joshu knew just as well as the monk that all beings without exception have buddha-nature, and thus we must not misinterpret Joshu's MU as a negation.

His only intention was to prevent the monk from wanting to understand Zen through rational thinking. Instead, he should be striving towards that higher perception of reality, "beyond affirmation and negation," in which all contradictions melt away of their own accord.

The essence when dealing with a →koan is that the Zen practitioner achieve that crystal-clear state of consciousness, from which the words were spoken and which logical analysis can never reach. Only when the student's mind has sufficiently matured to the stage where it is completely congenial with the master's mind who gave him the koan, will the profound truth reveal itself which was hidden within the koan. (see also →koan).

Mudra Sanskrit, a special posture of the hands with symbolic meaning.

Mumonkan Jap., literally: "The gateless gate". Alongside the →Pi-yen-lu, the most important collection of koans in Zen Buddhism (→Zen). It contains a collection of 48 →koans, compiled by Zen Master Mumon (thirteenth century) and accompanied by short Zen explanations.

Munen Jap. (Chin. Wu-nien); "Non-thinking, non-consciousness". Munen and →Mushin together form one of the central concepts of Zen.

Mushin Jap., (Chin. Wu-hsin); "Non-thinking, non-consciousness, seclusion of the mind". A natural state of mind entirely without aim, beyond all thought. In Zen, Munen does not mean ignorance or spiritual stupor but rather that the mind is so steadfast within itself that it cannot be perturbed by external circumstances, no matter what they may be.

Mushotoku Jap., without aim and striving for gain.

Nembutsu Jap. (Chin. Nien-fo), invocation of the name of →buddha →Amitabha. The western meditation form of the Buddhist school of the Pure Land (→Pure Land School). The invocation recited is "Namu Amida Butsu" (Jap. for "homage to the buddha Amitabha"). Nembutsu recited in complete faith and absolute devotion leads to reincarnation in Sukhavati, the western paradise of the buddha Amitabha.

Nirvana Sanskrit, literally: "extinguishment". The state of complete liberation (→Enlightenment), as opposed to →samsara, imprisonment in the cycle of birth and death. The Zen Buddhist does not view nirvana as separate from the world but as a state of consciousness in which one fulfils one's true being and thus surpasses suffering.

Non-mind→Mushin

OM ancient holy Indian symbol. It is one of the most important →mantras in →Tantric Buddhism, which is spread across the whole of the East. It stands for the all-encompassing, all-pervading presence of the Absolute in the universe. It is the divine original tone, which reflects the beginning and the essence of the entire cosmos as vibrations. (See also →mantra and →OM MANI PADME HUM)

OM MANI PADME HUM Sanskrit, literally: "→OM, jewel (in the) lotus, HUM". Invocation form for the →Bodhisattva →Avalokiteshvara. In this →mantra, "OM" and "HUM" stand for the beginning and the end, and symbolise totality. The meaning of "Jewel in the lotus" comes from the sameness of the jewel and the spirit of enlightenment (→Bodhichitta), with the wish to awaken it in the lotus of the consciousness. The Tibetans repeat this mantra constantly in order to strengthen their own devotion and affinity with Avalokiteshvara, the Bodhisattva of compassion.

Pi-yen-lu Chin., literally: "Blue Cliff Record," Jap. Hekigan-roku. The most important collection of koans in Zen Buddhism (→Zen) alongside the →Mumonkan. It was published in the twelfth century by the Chinese Zen Master Yuan-wu, one of the most significant masters in the history of Zen. It involves a collection of 100 →koans which, together with additional texts, belong to the zenith of the whole of Zen literature.

Prajna Sanskrit, literally: "Wisdom" (Pali: Panna, Jap. Hannya). In →Mahayana Buddhism Prajna is intuitively experienced insight into the voidness (→Shunyata) of all phenomena. Prajna is one of the principle characteristics of Buddhahood.

Pratitya-Samutpada Sanskrit, literally: "Emergence in mutual conditionality and dependence". The doctrine of the chain of conditional emergence is the foundation of all Buddhist schools. A deeper understanding of Buddhism depends on one's grasp of this doctrine. The Pratitya-Samutpada shows that all phenomena have no more than an empirical validity and are thus devoid of reality. All phenomena exist respectively in a causal and conditional relationship of dependence on each other and to each other. Nothing is to be found which is non-dependant and which has an existence out of itself.

Pure Land (Chin. Ching-tu, Jap. Jodo) →Sukhavati

Pure Land School → Amitabha

Rinzai School (Chin. Lin-chi-tsung, Jap. Rinzai-shu). Alongside the → Soto school, one of the predominant schools of Zen Buddhism (→ Zen) in Japan. The striking feature of Rinzai is the systematic use of → koans for gaining enlightenment (→ Satori).

Roshi Jap., literally: "old, venerable master". Original title of a Zen master. In times of old a Zen monk could only gain this title with great difficulty. It was only bestowed on those who had been acknowledged as having fulfilled → buddha dharma by way of directly experiencing it, and who were able to carry it over into everyday life. Total enlightenment (→ Satori) and a mature personality with a steadfast character were the necessary prerequisites. Today, true, completely enlightened Zen masters in Japan are extremely rare. The term "Roshi" has now been reduced to a general title for a Zen teacher, regardless of whether monk or layman. In respect of their age and position, monks are often addressed as "Roshi," so that this term is now empty and meaningless.

Samadhi Sanskrit (Jap. Sanmai or Zanmai), literally: "to fasten, to fix". A state of non-intentionality and freedom from thoughts. It is the state of focussing on a single object, brought about by calming the activity of the mind. In this non-dualistic state of consciousness the person meditating and the object of meditation become completely one. All dualism and the belief in a self, existing of itself and separate from everything else are overcome in Samadhi. However, this state of consciousness of Samadhi, free of all thinking, is neither numb nor unfeeling. Quite the contrary, it is crystal-clear awareness of mind.

Samantabhadra →Adi-Buddha

Samsara Sanskrit, literally: "roaming". The cycle of birth and death. The aim of all Buddhists and Hinduists is liberation from samsara, and thus from suffering. It is liberation from the imprisonment in the wheel of birth, ageing, despair, illness, pain and death.

Sat-Chit-Ananda Sanskrit, literally: "Being (Sat), consciousness (Chit), bliss (Ananda)". In →Vedanta, this term represents the experience gained through enlightenment of the inexpressible truth of the Absolute, →Brahman, as absolute being, boundless consciousness and bliss.

Satori Jap. (Chin. Wu). Zen term for the experience of enlightenment, or awakening. Satori is far more than an intuitive understanding of true being, as in the experience of →Kensho, since the person who experiences Satori dissolves entirely into it. In →Zen, Satori is described as the rebirth of the true Self once the false, illusory self; the ego-delusion has died the "Great Death".

Sesshin Jap., literally: "Concentration of the Heart-Mind". Intensive →zazen sitting periods lasting several days in total, interspersed with speeches by the master and the opportunity of a one-to-one talk (Dokusan).

Shastra Sanskrit, literally "textbook, instruction".

Shikantaza Jap., "Just sitting". →Soto school

Shoshin Jap., "Beginner's mind". The necessary state of mind of a Zen student for Zen instruction by a master. It is the attitude of mind in which the student recognises that he knows nothing. It is the absolute prerequisite for letting go of everything that sense and reason can comprehend.

Sunyata Sanskrit (Jap. Ku), literally: "emptiness,

void". According to the teachings of Mahayana nothing possesses a self-dependent, lasting substance. All things are empty and thus without self-nature. The teaching of sunyata is one of the cornerstones of the whole of →Mahayana Buddhism and accordingly of →Zen. It is very subtle and cannot be expressed in words. Although there is extensive literature covering this subject, sunyata is only completely understandable to those who have experienced it themselves it in the experience of enlightenment (→Satori).

Skandha Sanskrit (Pali: Khandha) "group, aggregate". In Buddhism, the five groups which constitute and define the human personality as it is commonly known.
Corporeality or form (Rupa)
Sensation (Vedana)
Perception (Samjna)
Mental formations (Samakara)
Consciousness (Vijnana)
What we commonly view as our personality is in truth nothing more than a process of interaction between these phenomena, which means that our "person" is no more than a sum of nonpersonal factors of existence.

Soto School (Chin. Tsao-tung-tsung, Jap. Soto-shu). Alongside the →Rinzai school, one of the two principle schools of Zen Buddhism (→Zen) in Japan. As opposed to Rinzai, Soto does not make use of →koans but rather, it practises a form of Zen comprised exclusively of just-sitting →Shikantaza, literally: "nothing but sitting". Since it insists on putting zazen on a par with enlightenment (→Satori), Soto is known as "silent enlightenment Zen".

Sukhavati Sanskrit, "blissful," the western paradise, ruled by →buddha →Amitabha. Reincarnation in Sukhavati paradise has the effect that one can no longer fall back into a reincarnation elsewhere(→Nembutsu).

Sung-Dynasty Chinese epoch, 960-1278

Sutra Sanskrit, literally "guideline". Sutras are the most important texts in Buddhism. Most of the sutras are instructive talks by →Buddha. In →Mahayana Buddhism many additional sutras were written after the Buddha's death and are regarded as being authoritative. They emerged between the first century B.C. and the sixth century A.D.

Tang-Dynasty Chinese epoch, 618-906; the period in which Zen Buddhism was at its peak (→Zen).

Tantrayana →Vajrayana

Tantric Buddhism →Vajrayana

Tao Chin., literally: "Way," central metaphysical term of →Taoism. Tao is the Absolute, the fundamental all-encompassing principle; the ultimate truth. Tao forms the core of Lao-tse's →Tao Te King and the teachings of Chuang-tse. The aim of all Taoists is to live in unison with Tao. Intellectual understanding is not enough, instead it is a matter of fulfilling the unity, simplicity and →voidness of Tao. "Action without intent", →Wu-wei, literally: Non-action, is seen as the principal attitude of mind of a Taoist.

Taoism There are two main streams of Taoism – the philosophical stream: Tao-chia, and the religious stream: Tao-chiao. Tao-chia dates back to the Taoist master Lao-tse and his book, the →Tao Te King. Here, acting without intent in unison with →Tao is seen as the highest ideal. On the other hand, the aim of the religious Taoism is physical immortality. It is to be achieved through breathing exercises, physical exercises and certain sexual practices.

Tao Te King Chin., literally: "The book of Tao and True Virtue". A work from the sixth century B.C. ascribed to the old Taoist master Lao-tse. It comprises five thousand characters and is therefore also known as "the book of the five thousand characters". The Tao Te King is the cornerstone of →Taoism and at the same time one of the most important and most translated books of world literature. The author of the Tao Te King must seem concealed and mysterious to us, just like the Tao of which he speaks. Lao-tse is said to have reached a very old age of well over a hundred years. He lived in Tschou, but as he saw that it was in the process of decaying he departed. On arriving at the border pass he encountered the border guard Yin Hsi, who recognised the master and begged him to leave behind something in writing. Thereupon, Lao-Tse wrote his book, the Tao Te King in which he expressed his thoughts on Tao and true virtue. Subsequently, riding on his buffalo, he departed. No one knows what became of him.

The Tao Te King teaches us to follow the "Way of Heaven," to practice non-action →Wu-wei and thus to allow the force of true virtue to act in us. For heaven is without action yet causes all things, Wei-wu-wei, literally: Acting non action. Whoever lives in such unison with the harmonic transformation of heaven becomes a revelation of Tao in the world and achieves immortality beyond death.

Tathata Sanskrit, "Thusness, thus-being, that which is". A core concept of →Mahayana Buddhism. It describes the Absolute, the true nature of all things. Tathata is beyond all dualistic concepts, it is unchanging and the opposite of all apparent phenomena. As the thusness of all things it is formless, uncreated and without self-nature. It is identical to →buddha-nature and thus equivalent to the →dharmakaya.

Tathagata Sanskrit, literally "The one who has thus gone (thus arrived there, thus come)". This term is used as an honorary title to express Buddha's identity as a consummate being. As a perfectly enlightened →buddha he acts as a mediator between the Absolute and the world of phenomena.

Te Chin., literally: "virtue, power". The spiritual force of the →Tao, as revealed to those who live in unison with the Tao. Lao-Tse calls "Te" true virtue in his Tao Te King. It is what can be called spontaneous experience through Tao.

Tibetan Buddhism →Vajrayana

Upanishads Sanskrit: Upanishad, literally: "to sit close by," i.e. to sit near to the master to receive the secret teachings. The Upanishads are a category of texts that make up the final part of the Veda and are the fundamental basis of →Advaita-Vedanta. They are concerned with ultimate truth and belong to the holy revelation scriptures of Hinduism.

Vajra Sanskrit (Tib.: Dorje); "diamond," diamond sceptre. Symbol for the indestructibility of the void (→Shunyata), as the true being and the essence of all that is.

Vajrayana Sanskrit, literally: "diamond vehicle," often known as Tantric Buddhism, also as Tibetan Buddhism. In Vajrayana, the practitioner works creatively with the force of imagination given to him by his master. This takes place through use of visualisation and →mantras, by identifying himself with his →Yidam, a pictorial particular manifestation of a →buddha. For this reason, Buddha statues, Mandalas, and Thankas (iconographic representations) play a large role as a memory aid for visualisation in Tantric Buddhism.

Vajrayana-Buddhism Vajrayana

Vedanta Sanskrit Advaita-Vedanta

Void, emptiness →Shunyata

Wu Chin., literally: "Nothing, non-being". →Mu

Wu-hsin Chin. →Mushin

Wu-nien, Chin. →Munen

Wu-wei Chin., literally: "Non-action" in the sense of "action without acting". This Taoist term is not to be confused with passively doing nothing. Much rather, it means the attitude of mind of non-intervention in the natural course of things. In truth, Wu-wei is a highly effective state of mind, in which any action is possible at any time. By living non-action, the Taoist sage is in unison with Tao, whose universal power is brought to bear exactly due to this non-action. The great Taoist master of old, Lao-tse thus says in his →Tao Te King: Tao is eternally without action, but nothing remains undone.

Wu-Wei is therefore a matter of creative non-action, an actless conduct which underlies the mental attitude of non-intervention and the courage of letting things happen. Wu-Wei transcends both extremes – restless activity and absolute inactivity. It is a non-action of the unimportant, which at the same time allows the essential to take effect.

Yamantaka Sanskrit →Manjushri

Yidam Sanskrit →Vajrayana

Zanmai Jap. →Samadhi

Zazen Jap. (Chin. Tsao-chan), literally: "sitting in immersion," the common meditation practice in →Zen. All great masters of Zen view zazen as a practice which is indispensable and fundamental in Zen. Zazen is abiding of the mind in a state of crystal-clear awareness, free of content and not focussed on any object.

Zen Jap., an abbreviation of "Zenna," the Japanese way of reading the Chinese "channa" (in short, chan), which itself is a transcript of the Sanskrit word "Dhyana". Zen-Buddhism developed in the 6th and 7th centuries in China from the combination of Bodhidarma's transmission of Indian Dhyana-Buddhism and Chinese Taoism. Characteristic of Zen is its particularly strong emphasis on the experience of enlightenment (→Satori). Integral to Zen is also the development of intuitive comprehension through meditation (→zazen) instead of intellectual studies.

In the ninth century the Chinese Zen masters developed a new teaching method. From then on, the masters made use of paradoxical phrases (→koans) in order for their students to gain an understanding of the truth beyond discriminating, conceptual thinking. Here, they often employed violent methods, such as hitting, kicking or shouting to open the eye of enlightenment of their students. From the 12th century onwards the Zen masters called on their students to concentrate on a koan for so long until they reached enlightenment.

The two main schools of thought in Zen are Rinzai and Soto-Zen. Rinzai is characterised by its koan practice, whereas Soto emphasises more the importance of sitting meditation (→zazen).

The fundamental characteristics of Zen were summarized in the early →Tang-Dynasty in four short statements in Chinese:

1. Transmission outside the orthodox teachings
2. Independence from holy scriptures
3. Directly pointing towards the "Heart-Mind"
4. Perception of one's own nature and attainment of Buddhahood

Contact

ZEN CENTER
TAO 道禅 CHAN

Tao Chan Zentrum e.V.
Non-profit society
Wiesbaden, Germany

Twice a month, the Zen Center Tao Chan organises a Zen-evening with a talk by Zen Master Zensho W. Kopp, where guests are welcome to attend. There is also the possibility for asking Zen Master Zensho questions. More information at: www.tao-chan.org

Register here for the evening:

www.tao-chan.org/events/events-zen-night.html

Subscribe here for free short talks by Zen Master Zensho W. Kopp:

www.youtube.com/@zencentertaochan/shorts
www.youtube.com/@zencentertaochan

Facebook site for the Zen Center Tao Chan

www.facebook.com/zencentertaochan

Instagram: www.instagram.com/zenmasterzensho/

TikTok: www.tiktok.com/@zenmaster_zensho.w.kopp

Books by Zensho W. Kopp

also available as eBook Kindle Edition

Order here: www.tao-chan.org/zen-master-zensho/books.html

The immortality of the true self

Printed book: 108 pages, 11.90 €

· Also as Kindle Edition

Living in inner fullness

Printed book: 116 pages, 9.80 €

· Also as Kindle Edition

The power of inner quietude

Printed book: 104 pages, 9.80 €

· Also as Kindle Edition

Now is Eternity

Printed book: 114 pages, 9.80 €

· Also as Kindle Edition

The light of wisdom
Printed book: 114 pages, 13.50 €

· Also as Kindle Edition

The radiating clarity
of the mind
Printed book: 136 pages, 12.95 €

· Also as Kindle Edition

The ascent of
the inner Light
Printed book: 114 pages, 11.99 €

· Also as Kindle Edition

The Flame
of Awareness
Printed book: 124 pages, 12.90 €

· Also as Kindle Edition

The mystery of
true self-recognition
Printed book: 128 pages, 13.90 €

· Also as Kindle Edition

Books by Zensho W. Kopp
also available as eBook, audiobooks or download

The Freedom of Zen

The Zen book that shatters all
limits and bounds
Printed book: 154 pages, 12.95 €

· Audiobook (CD)
· MP3 download
· Kindle Edition

Awakening the heart-mind

ZEN in daily life
Printed book: 187 pages, 9.99 €

· Audiobook (CD)
· MP3 download
· Kindle Edition

Words of the Awakened Mind

Aphorisms of a Western Zen Master
Printed book: 140 pages, 9.95 €

· Kindle Edition

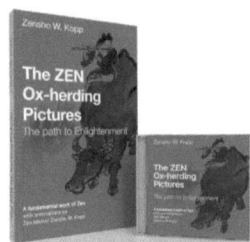

The ZEN Ox-herding Pictures

The path to Enlightenment
Printed book: 212 pages, 9.95 €

· Audiobook (CD)
· MP3 download
· Kindle Edition

Lao-tse – Tao Te King

The Book of Tao and Spiritual Force
Printed book: 120 pages , 9.95 €

· Audiobook (CD)
· MP3 download
· Audible audiobook
· Kindle Edition

True Life Through Zen

Spiritual self-realisation in daily life
Printed book: 140 pages, 11.50 €

· Audiobook (CD)
· MP3 download
· Audible audiobook
· Kindle Edition

Awakening to Your True SELF

The Zen way of all-embracing mysticism
Printed book: 140 pages, 11.99 €

· Audiobook (CD)
· MP3 download
· Audible audiobook
· Kindle Edition

The direct Zen-Way to Liberation

A profound wisdom which
transforms and liberates
Printed book: 212 pages

· Audiobook (CD)
· MP3 download
· Audible audiobook
· Kindle Edition

Modern ZEN-ART
Watercolours and sayings of a
Western Zen Master

DE / EN

Printed book: 136 pages, 23.50 €

Enlightened Dimensions of the Divine
Paintings and quotations of a
Western Zen Master

Printed book: 144 pages, 10.50 €

All publications by Zensho can be found and purchased here:
www.tao-chan.org/zen-master-zensho/books.html